I'm very into you

Published by Semiotext(e)
PO BOX 629, South Pasadena, CA 91031
www.semiotexte.com

The editor would like to thank the late, great Chiasmus Press: Andy Mingus, Trevor Dodge & particularly Lidia Yuknavitch. This project began its journey with them and will always bear their mark. Also heartfelt thanks to Ken Goffman, aka RU Sirius, Sylvère Lotringer, Chris Kraus, Hedi El Kholti & McKenzie Wark for his courage in all things.

Cover shows the ring given to Ken Wark by Kathy Acker in New York City, September 1995. The ring was designed by Alex Streeter.
The photograph is by Arturo Cubria.

Design: Hedi El Kholti

ISBN: 978-1-58435-164-1
Distributed by The MIT Press, Cambridge, Mass. and London, England
Printed in the United States of America
10 9 8 7

I'm very into you

Correspondence 1995–1996

Kathy Acker | McKenzie Wark

Edited and with an Introduction by Matias Viegener

Afterword by John Kinsella

semiotext(e)

PORTISHEADSPACE

Here before you is the surviving correspondence between Kathy Acker and McKenzie Wark. These emails were hastily written, casual and often indirect; they crossed "in the mail" and both the sequence and references may confuse the reader. The authors barely knew each other, the correspondence lasts a little over two weeks, and their relationship lasted only a few weeks beyond the last of the letters. You might ask why publish them at all, and so did I, but only after a novelist Ken Wark and I (and Kathy Acker) held in great esteem turned down our request for a preface. Initially very enthusiastic, on closer reading the novelist found the letters too personal. In declining, the novelist said it felt too much like rooting around in someone's underwear drawer.

Is this a terrible mistake? I pulled back to reconsider. I reread everything. The letters are personal, but they tell us only a little about the author's lives. Many of the things they reveal you can easily find in these writers' published works. They gossip a little about their friends, some famous and some not, but all of them interesting. Most of the content rests on what they are thinking about rather than how they feel, on their questions for each other, and on what they are reading, rather than what other people have said or done. In part the letters read like bibliographies or indexes, chock full of cultural referents that map the correspondents within their literary, critical and pop cultural eras. They talk a lot about sex, about gender roles, about drag unveiled and re-ironized for familiar purpose: to flirt.

These letters mark the passage of two people in a brief moment in time. If you wanted to know how brainy nerds of a certain period fall into courtship, this is your book. Ken Wark and Kathy Acker met in Sydney in July of 1995 and this is the email exchange that followed. To call them love letters would exaggerate their tenor and consequence, but there is an irresistible tug of seduction in them. Not love letters, but certainly letters of intention: the narrative advances indirectly, thrusts and parries, messages get confused and reach an impasse. This is only broken when Acker finally confesses she's "very into" Ken Wark. If paper letters were best suited for love, perhaps email does best with crushes. What you have before you is not the artifact of an affair, but of a seduction. Of what happens after the letters end, perhaps Ken Wark will speak if he chooses. Suffice it to say here that they saw each other a few more times but that other things intervened, and that two long years later Kathy Acker was dead from cancer.

Lest you think this is a record of Kathy Acker's last stab at love, it isn't. That happens a year later, though it left fewer remnants. Sexual desire, seduction and romantic obsessions are at the core of many of Acker's texts, just as they formed a through-line in her life. She filtered her daily life throughout her manuscripts. This wasn't ancillary to her work; it was its very fiber.

> I call up D in Los Angeles do you want to sleep with me with me when and where there why don't you spend a few days with me I'll call you tomorrow. No call three days later I'm maniacal I have to see D I don't know him hello I've got a ride to Los Angeles lie I'm not sure I know where we can stay should I not come up come up. We don't touch talk about anything personal until we get to motel never talk about anything personal spend night together I have to be at Irvine in the morning I'm busy call me Friday. Do you want me to call you yes. I call Friday call Saturday Sunday this is Kathy O uh do you want to spend a night with me again are you too busy uh goodbye have a good time in New York uh goodbye. [*The Childlike Life of the Black Tarantula*, in *Portrait of an Eye*, New York, Pantheon, 1992, p.4.]

Two paragraphs past the opening of Black Tarantula, Acker bursts through the appropriated narrative of the murderess Charlotte Wood by appropriating her own found material, and of course, her lover's. It's an early instance linking the power of plagiarism and the force of transgression in her work. This mining of autobiographical information persisted throughout her life, and led many readers to irrepressible ideas about who she was or what she wanted. Early in her career, Acker not only didn't discourage this, but actively deployed both her life and her body in a sort of performative

(7)

persona. This persona succeeded rather well in attracting readers, but also generated a set of problems in strangers who confused the persona with Kathy herself. This often annoyed her, because it became most acute when she was interested in a lover.

When she was not preceded by her persona, she was often preceded by her work. Early in their emails, Wark mentions that he's opened one of Acker's books at random, and types out the passage:

> Hot female flesh on hot female flesh. And it doesn't go anywhere: flesh. Flesh. For the cunt opens and closes, a perpetual motion machine, a scientific wonder, perpetually coming, opening and closing on itself to ecstasy or nausea—does it, you, ever tire? Roses die faster. Roses die faster than you, you whores in my heart. [*Empire of the Senseless*, p. 141]

He reveals that he'd read *Empire of the Senseless* five years earlier, and marked it with a pencil, a passage in which Thivai reflects on the loss of love to sex. After he notes its qualities, the contrast of beauty and violence, and its bittersweet tension, he reflects on Acker's presence (or absence) in the text. "I imagine I can sense you hiding, a perpetual motion machine in my hands, between the lines. There are reaches of me that I can only put in language as feminine, and those reaches exposed themselves to you, felt comfortable next to you sometimes." The perpetual motion machine in his hands is as much the keyboard as the image of his correspondent, and corresponds in turn to the frenzy of transcription in Acker's own early work: everything is put in, nothing is excluded. In the exchange between Acker and Wark, we see the reciprocal machinery of projection and introjection.

Like others before him, Wark reads Acker through her work, but unlike them he consciously monitors his own process of transference and introjection. As the correspondence evolves there is a tango of reading, recognition, misreading and self-recognition. Each has an idealized self he or she wishes to project on the other, and each scrutinizes how he or she has been misrecognized by the world and then reveals his machinations for further drag subterfuge. Wark confesses his own form of masochism and his desire to be a public whipping boy on a larger scale than he (yet) is. He recognizes the power of misrecognition and also his own longing for it. There's a queer energy here moving in more than two directions.

Earlier on, Wark questions his confessional tendencies. "Why am I telling you all this? Partly 'cause the whole queerness/identity thing for me stretches through everything, absolutely everything. Slipping between straight/gay is child's play compared to slipping between writer/teacher/influence-peddler whatever. I forget who I am. You reminded me of who I prefer to be." Perhaps the oblique reference to the slippage between them is to age, the fourteen-year age difference between a man of 34 and a woman of 48. The emails often return to this question in the guise of asking who is learning more from whom. Acker and Wark both prefer laying claim to the role of the student, and their correspondence is laced by the passage of information from one to the other, by questions nearly held back and answers given with lavish care. The question of translation runs from American to Australian through butch and femme back home through Continental philosophy mashed up against *The Simpsons*.

Many of Acker's lovers were older than her, intellectual men like Peter Wollen and Sylvère Lotringer, whose role as teachers were invariably complicated by the varieties of resistance that arose in consequence. Even Acker's relations with men the same age were loaded with yearning for knowledge. In 1973, Acker and Alan Sondheim made a video together that documents the collapse of their courtship. *The Blue Tape* is a counterpoint to the Acker/Wark correspondence, a set of bittersweet monologues on each lover's disappointment in the other, his intellectual and hers erotic. While it appears 22 years before these letters, it is a kind of postscript to the failure of writing, as Acker and Sondheim both refer to the letters they wrote to each other to arrange their rendezvous in New York. It's a fugue of affliction. The video ends in silence, as Acker prints out her frustrations with squeaky chalk on a blackboard.

All intimate letters share a seductive function, with words in place of gestures and images in place of bodies. The struggle for intimacy in these letters is also a struggle with intimacy, with the uncertainty of whether it is better or easier to desire or be desired. Neither position is easy for our correspondents, and they trade their cards again and again. Even as they seduce, both Acker and Wark express their desire to be seduced.

We find a yearning to be understood in Acker's words quite different from those of her novel's narrators. Perhaps it's the realization at middle age that the persona she so carefully scripted and performed might have an afterlife not entirely in her own control. As one would expect, she wants this new relationship to be between her and her interlocutor, not between Kathy Acker and

McKenzie Wark. But from the earliest letters she is preceded by her image. In order to undo this precedence she must write more, or unwrite and rewrite herself. There is a weird logic of the supplement at work here, because each articulation asks to be read both for itself and cumulatively. Revision and rewriting get re-cast in dizzying citationality: you'll find a veritable millennial bibliography, inflected through the iconoclasm of these two writers.

Acker is very interested in the Ken Wark who had just published *Virtual Geography*, a study of the impact of the media on the experience of the everyday. It evokes a world in which aerials replace roots and terminals replace origins, and it laid the groundwork of his subsequent books. The narrative conventions of the media turn wars into video games and make everyday reality a mediated presence in which the reporter himself is interviewed to fully convey the event at hand, a phenomenon Wark buttons up by disclosing how he himself is implicated as viewer or reader.

Like *The Blue Tape* in the 70s, this correspondence is a symptomology of how two educated people from a certain artistic, critical and political milieu of the 90s seduce each other: through critical theory and pop culture references. As a document of its time, it shows us a cultural moment of strange harmonies between high theory and low culture, a lingua franca set into place by the confluence of Continental philosophy, psychoanalysis and post-Marxist cultural studies. Among the things they talk about are William Burroughs, Hitchcock, Gurdjieff, stuffed animals, the music of Portishead, the cards of the *I Ching*, Todd Hayne's *Safe*, science fiction and action adventure blockbusters, Alphonso Lingis' phenomenology, the television era of the *X-Files*, *The*

Simpsons, and *Beavis and Butthead*; the novels of Elfriede Jelinek, the work of Spinoza, Baudrillard, Judith Butler, Bataille, Blanchot, Plato, and Nietzsche; the icons of Elvis Presley, Warhol and Pier Paolo Pasolini. There is a burning urgency to their grand and fine articulations of difference: these are thinkers who live in citation, critical theory, popular culture, sex, drugs, and rock and roll. Both Wark and Acker are engineering their alterity, yearning for the possibility of radical otherness. Rimbaud's originary "I am an other" becomes "we are others, even to ourselves."

The butch/femme dialectic pervades their exchanges even more than the continuum between straight and gay to queer. Some future anthropologist will note our preoccupation with these distinctions, perhaps with bemusement, tracing the role of Judith Butler's *Gender Trouble* in establishing the queer as the last ethical position in the cavalcade of the sexual revolution. Both Wark and Acker yearn for a tenable category of desiring self, regardless of one's historic sexual orientation. They discuss the nature of love, like Plato's *Symposium*, fascinated with queers, lesbians and gay men, with alternative models—if not utopian then at least more mindful ones. Redefining sexuality beyond bisexuality, identity is no longer a useful rubric in terms of sexuality. For Wark equality, "in the sense of the double, the exact equal, is a myth. So the ethical question is: how can difference remain fluid, open?" Between these two we witness a sweet and lyrical tango on gender, which culminates in Wark telling Acker she's a better man than he is. And yet though masculinity becomes a kind of drag, in this duet it is still the feminine that bears all the emotion, certainly all of the doubt, or rather: the woman who externalizes the emotion, and the doubt. She raises the emotional questions, culminated not by a question mark but a period, an apostrophe, an ejaculation: *I'm very into you.*

Emotions however are quickly deposed by speculation, intellectual play set free from the constraints of academic discourse. They're in the stew of 20th century critical theory, from French poststructuralism to gender studies to the Germans. The speculative heat comes to a head when Acker and Wark start examining Blanchot's unavowable community in relation to Bataille's use of transgression. Concepts such as these are set into play against each other and roll off the platform just in time for the next volley of philosophic word games. But the *telos* here fittingly begins (and ends) in the non-place of the airport and the airplane. Though this volume begins and ends in airports, the internet is its real site, perfectly pitched against the spacious, echoing soundtrack of Portishead.

Yet within this contemporary site, we essentially arrive at the quaint form of the epistolary novel. Unlike within the novel of letters, innocence isn't lost here, but remade over and again. It's the tracings of two cynics who want to believe. Two people staring down a death culture while yearning to affirm the joy of life. Their problem is that they know too much, but also know that this knowledge protects them from nothing.

This is a text about transit and transition. Both correspondents want to write something into being, a conjuration. But there's no ending here. Wark tells me that the emails stop just before he left Sydney to travel to New York, stopping in San Francisco to visit Acker, after which they both travelled to New

York and spent a little more time together at the Gramercy Hotel. There were emails between them after, but of these only one survives, and it ends this volume. Hence most of the actual encounter, Wark's term, rather than affair, is absent. They met for the last time in the final year of Acker's life, in London, after her mastectomy for the breast cancer that later killed her. As Wark remembers it, they went to see a performance piece by an HIV+ gay man, who told the story of his subsumption into the machinery of medicalization. The piece took place in the morgue beneath an old hospital, and ended with him lying on a table as if dead, in the "viewing room" for relatives of the deceased. I mention this here to emphasize the tragic weight of Acker's death, which still hovers over all those who knew her.

It was strange to edit this, and to chose to publish it. I found my own name misspelled in the manuscript, and corrected it, and have also altered the names of a few individuals whose privacy I believe Acker would not have wanted compromised. Wark has also changed some names. There's an intensity here forged in part by the medium itself, the then new medium of email. Today's reader will notice the writer's occasional references to a technology which has entirely naturalized itself for us. It has a speculative, asynchronous quality at odds with the immediacy we now associate with email. It's a text of incipience, a text of beginnings, a set of notes on the short, shared passage of two remarkable and iconic individuals of our time. I thank Ken Wark for agreeing to publish, for his fearless commitment to intensity, contradiction and emotional truth. I'm sure Acker would never have agreed to their publication were she alive, but she is dead. What is it exactly that an executor does, other than answer queries and sign contracts? Perhaps we will know her differently now, and him as well. A dead writer can only exist in words, and I publish these letters less in the spirit of total revelation than total text: everything in Acker's life was text, including her death. She visited me in the middle of this correspondence, and later sent me an email about Ken—which like much email is lost in the ether, more like the fate of all speech rather than writing. And so dear reader, though these words were not addressed to you, I hope you now find them in your lap with at least some of the electricity with which they were generated.

Correspondence 1995–1996

Date: Tue, 8 Aug 1995 00:14:31 +1000 (EST)
From: McKenzie Wark <mwark@laurel.ocs.mq.edu.au>
To: Kathy Acker <acker@eworld.com>
Subject: greetings from hooterville

I drove out of the airport in a daze and motored straight out to work. After shuffling papers around on my desk like a jigsaw puzzle I came home and slept all day. Hadn't realised how much of a compound hangover hung over. It's now late Monday night and I'm feeling better. Been reading alternate chapters of _Exterminator!_ and the Bockris bio of Warhol. You were absolutely right about the Burroughs. The second chapter is about 'becoming wolf.' I feel a bit like there was some kind of napalm strike and I missed it. There's not much I can say 'cause whatever happened I don't seem to have been a witness. Or maybe like Gregory Peck in _Spellbound_, it'll come back to me.

But I certainly won't forget that I enjoyed being with you. The shared intimacies of body, mind and spirit: it's such a fleeting thing, so singular. I think we're probably both pretty solitary in our own ways, but for a slice out of time we were singular together. There are no words. I just want to say there are no words. I'm glad you came; and I'm glad you came. Thinking about you sleeping on a plane with those knockout herbal sleep-bombs of yours. Bear with me. I'll have something to say for myself sometime soon. When I remember who I thought I was in the first place. Even if I've been displaced a little from wherever that was.

kxx

Date: Mon, 7 Aug 1995 19:13:00 -0700
From: Acker@eworld.com
To: mwark@laurel.ocs.mq.edu.au
Subject: Re: greetings from hooterville

It's so great coming home to your message, more precisely, coming home to find out that luggage was missing until the next plane, then the checks I got in Australia for work all can't be cashed 'cause they're non-negotiable and I have ten dollars in the bank, and then and then, oh jetlag, so your message is changing the day—or is it night?—around. Whatever in virtual or non-virtual the sky, and Gurdjieff made the plane bearable (reading him, an adventure story, imagine that), so I too—this was all a long prelude—am terribly dazed, about to fall into the bath and then try to write, fuck food—and dazed a bit still about meeting you…but truly glad…you have a rare delicacy and grace, Ken, in all aspects…all the time there (in Sydney) that I didn't know what was going on and so would begin to become confused and so paranoid, and even now, what becomes/became present was how easy it is to be with you. Like: you the one I want/wanted to talk to. Thank you. Yes, there's always solitude but, for me, I am even more grateful when there are meetings. Oh. I'll recede, not into confusion, but pure tiredness now (the bath) and Portishead…look for new books to read…talk to my stuffed animals…began reading your _Virtual Geography_ on the plane…shall write again when more coherent…byebye (like, lullabye)

Date: Wed, 9 Aug 1995 01:46:51 +1000 (EST)
From: McKenzie Wark <mwark@laurel.ocs.mq.edu.au>
To: Acker@eworld.com
Subject: portisheadspace

Tuesday night. Put the Portishead on. I'll associate it with you now. Funny how music becomes an external memory code.

I hope yr bath was a pleasant one. What are your stuffed animals called? Bummer about the checks (or as one would write here, cheques). Asynchronous conversation.

Strange, trying to translate an understanding of communication premised on your presence into one premised on yr absence—writing.

But it's not a good idea to get too self-conscious…

I'm in an abstract state of mind. Just wrote a multimedia policy for the department. Thinking about how the resource allocation can be used to drive certain desired outcomes. Power trippin', in other words. Tomorrow I get to meet the prime minister and cabinet. I'm tagging along to a meeting about access issues in new media. Power voyeurism, in other words. I'm in it so I can put the scene in my next book.

Why am I telling you all this? Partly 'cause the whole queerness/ identity thing for me stretches through everything, absolutely everything. Slipping between straight/gay is child's play compared to slipping between writer/teacher/influence-peddler whatever. I forget who I am. You reminded me of who I prefer to be.

Can the spots change their leopard?

Do we need to analyse our encounter with each other? Or can we just assume it, and see what kind of dialogue it anchors to a start in time?

I opened one of your books at random:

"Hot female flesh on hot female flesh. And it doesn't go anywhere: flesh. Flesh. For the cunt opens and closes, a perpetual motion machine, a scientific wonder, perpetually coming, opening and closing on itself to ecstasy or nausea—does it, you, ever tire? Roses die faster. Roses die faster than you, you whores in my heart."

And I notice that I marked this with a pencil the first time I read it, which must have been 5 year ago. The really beautiful, in the classical sense beautiful passages stand out so clearly because of the violence around them. It's like being the decadent count in Dali's novel, putting a drop of extreme sweetness on his tongue to balance the preceding drop of the quintessence of bitterness.

But now I imagine I can sense you hiding, a perpetual motion machine in my hands, between the lines. There are reaches of me that I can only put in language as feminine, and those reaches

(22)

exposed themselves to you, felt comfortable next to you sometimes. That doesn't happen very often.

But I'm starting to analyse: to put the digital of the word in the place of the ebb of memory.

To wind up with a stray thought: the I Ching for our times. Not the randomly chosen page of the same text, but the same page every day on a different text. Page 141. Every day, another page 141. The I Ching is a closed universe/text, but we need a divining mechanism for an open, endless one. A perpetual motion machine that moves differently each time. Will that which you would have return, always, differently.

kxx

Date: Wed, 9 Aug 1995 01:52:42 -0700
From: Acker@eworld.com
To: mwark@laurel.ocs.mq.edu.au
Subject: Re: portisheadspace

Oh will I remember all that you just wrote? Memory slips even more than…what?…gender (is that self? not here)…and I was going to email, I can't even remember spelling, to just quickly tell you about the movie I just saw, Todd Haynes _Safe_…and your email!…now I can't remember all you said 'cause I want to tell you, emotion taking over, see _Safe_, it is WONDERFUL hits the spot (advertisers

(23)

make correctness) makes the art world into the stupid nothing it is…well it is so great seeing something that good…I saw it with RU we're friends again which is great 'cause I hate losing friends there aren't enough and it is my family, my friends…so now all is dream…Australia and this usual life melding, here where I do my emailing at two in the morning and wake up figuring out deals business how to give my publisher his share of daily grief oh will I get enough hours to write? I'm so greedy to do that…not like Sydney passing days drunk roaming through the bookstore with you…oh no please "analysis"? For me, "analysis" means "Kathy's being insecure and needs to breathe a few times." I hate it and can't remember anything anyways…except dreams…all this reality slipping and sliding…my main stuffed animals are Gulfie otherwise known as Woofie who is a feral witch I mean wolf only I just washed him so he looks almost sweet which is very disconcerting but probably needs my stinky body next to his so he can become feral again…and then there's Ratski (Rat) the star of my new novel 'cause the pirate girls' banner is RAT EATS ALL (based on certain ways of telling about the "musa" (mouse) (rat according to me) who sits at Ganesh's feet) …and then there's WITCH or BITCH who is very powerful so I tongue kiss her a lot all my animals are very penetrable including my feral motorcycles…one is still in shop and the other needs a carb adjustment but is happy I'm back 'cause he needs a lot of attention from me…is this pantheism or just spaciness?…it's two in the morning…I know what you mean about slipping roles: I love it, going high low, power helpless even captive, male female, all over the place, space totally together and brain-sharp, if it wasn't for play I'd be bored stiff and I think boredom is the emotion I find most

(24)

unbearable...I'd say there's my love for Baudelaire but he's also so cool when he talks about Jeannne Duval's stinky body it makes me feel as if I'm in this danger whose name is sex...I know what you mean about slipping male/female I never know which one I am I used to get all worried about myself, I should make decisions, announce a name, and at some point I just gave up 'cause it's too difficult and, oh, I started this book by Alphonse Lingis _The Community Of Those Who Have Nothing In Common_, the title reminds me of Blanchot, the intro. is so great, as I was reading it I started seeing (thinking) what you said about ethics, the need...sort of the terrain of _Safe_...I love emailing you...last night when I went to bed I thought, oh it's strange doing this without K, what a great sudden feeling 'cause I never feel that and it's good to remember things like that again...like a sudden opening into a forgotten territory...emailing must be pure narcissism...I think I'm going to blab even more intensely now so byebye for tonight...I'm not good at saying things emotionally I guess that's one place I'm male, am pleased that you're better at it than me... I just get awkward when I should be direct and say, oh what do you think it all means? I also have a huge fat white cat who used to be the queen of the world because she was so aristocratic but now has been mashed by too much sleeping with me and looks like a rat though not feral I also have a shark but he stays in the living room 'cause he's not furry after all there are rules of proper behavior oh byebye

Date: Wed, 9 Aug 1995 19:43:59 +1000 (EST)
From: McKenzie Wark <mwark@laurel.ocs.mq.edu.au>
To: Acker@eworld.com
Subject: Re: portisheadspace

Greetings from Canberra, bureaucracy's answer to Disneyland. Like Washington, only even more provincial. It's a long distance call, so this is just to say hi. Watching new series _The Simpsons_—it's getting pretty weird. Gotta go investigate the minibar...
kxx

Date: Wed, 9 Aug 1995 23:26:56 -0700
From: Acker@eworld.com
To: mwark@laurel.ocs.mq.edu.au
Subject: Re: portisheadspace

Simpsons, huh? I'll check it out. Am depressed, a rarity for me, so want to blab a little. More: scream. Have already screamed at RU and my closest girlfriend here, Dianne. It's so cool: while I was away, she fell in love with this beautiful girl who owns the new fancy restaurant in town. Dianne's so happy. She's totally beautiful: won a few bodybuilding contests and works as a psychic (California life). I'm avoiding my scream. Oh, I usually feel narcissistic on email and just blab everything, but now I'm becoming shy. It's that damn Sylvère [Lotringer]. The moment his marriage breaks up, he phones me. A few months ago. Now he's in LA; phones me again. I ask, what's up. He tells me that he has the huge books coming on: a several-volume compilation of Foucault, one of Félix [Guattari's] works. Etc. A dream about Félix. Then begins talking about his wife/ex-wife, Chris Kraus. How she needs a boyfriend. Why? Because she wants to be happy (she left him). All well and fine. Finally, he asks about me and I don't want to say anything, paranoid, so I mumble something about being sick of teaching at an art college and wanting a decent univ. job with benefits. One always talks about such nonsense when one doesn't want to say anything. No, before this, Sylvère does his usual rap about the stupidity of Americans, their misunderstanding of French theory. Which always irritates me for obvious reasons. I reply something about identity, this crap about national identity, etc. He ignores my comment, as usual. OK, on to boring teaching. Sylvère, after I say I want a decent job, replies "You mean they haven't discovered you yet?" I don't know what he means by "discover," I think that maybe he's making some bad joke about no one knowing my writing. I ask him what he means by "discover." "Discovered that you're the Unabomber in San Francisco." I don't know if I can explain this but suddenly I saw, the way one sees into an opening, a large section of my past. Ten to fifteen years with Sylvère, on and off. That I had been treated like this, seen like this, then: that was my past. It was totally disgusting: that vision. I usually don't think about what I do (rationally): I mean, say to myself, I will now sleep with women rather than men 'cause men treat me like a piece of shit. I mean, one (you I) just does what one does. But suddenly I saw, this glimpse, why I had gotten away from straight men. Yuck. And always, every interview, I have always respected Sylvère and said, he taught me, he was very

(27)

important to me. Now, a past that has been seen and thrown away. To be without a past. Well. Well. Is this an awful thing to tell you? I mean, invading a kind of privacy, a privacy based on our not knowing each other that long? But then, we are getting to know each other. Well, hell, sometimes one can't look at some straight men too closely, for the sight causes too much anger. What a way to put it. I'm, not pissed, no, I'm sad. I want a past I can acknowledge. It's all awful. Oh well. Reading [Elfriede] Jelinek's new book tonight; it's quite fab. Have to fax my old agent; tell her about the new one; more working until midnight; what are you doing in Canberra? Is that part of the university dignitary business? Take care of yourself, honey. (We say "honey" in America though not in New York.)

Date: Thu, 10 Aug 1995 17:48:52 +1000 (EST)
From: McKenzie Wark <mwark@laurel.ocs.mq.edu.au>
To: Acker@eworld.com
Subject: Re: portisheadspace

Before I forget, I don't have yr address to mail the stuff from Tracey. Lemme know where you want me to send it.

That episode of the _Simpsons_ I watched was 28 minutes total critique of work, family, breeding, with 2 minutes tacked on the end defending the same. I love TV when it's like old Hollywood movies—in a state of complete narrative hypocrisy.

I was in Canberra for a meeting of The National Information Services Council, as part of the team reporting on access issues. Five members of cabinet, two departmental heads, 15 top bureaucrats and a partridge in a pear tree. I got to meet the prime minister, who opened the proceedings. He's so tiny! He's as slight as me and a bit shorter. Poor man wasn't well, so he ducked out after opening proceedings. This is how this country is run these days. Government flies in talent to talk up ideas, then looks it all over with a gimlet eye. My social democrat self actually believes in all this. My anarchist self took notes and laughed up its sleeve. It'll make a good scene for my next book.

I'm probably not a bad choice of person to whom to unburden yourself about Sylvère. I don't have any preconceptions and I'm a long way away. It sounds like *he's* the one with an identity problem. From your account it sounds like one of those things where he feels about an inch tall so he's making out like you're half an inch tall. It's interesting how the value of the past with someone depends on how much they keep faith with that shared past. Sounds like an unpleasant experience. Old friends should know better than to disappoint us! Makes us question ourselves as much as them, as there is a bit of them in us, us in them…

Date: Thu, 10 Aug 1995 22:58:17 +1000 (EST)
From: McKenzie Wark <mwark@laurel.ocs.mq.edu.au>
To: Acker@eworld.com
Subject: joe delassandro

I'm watching all the Warhol/Morrissey films I can get, one after another. God joe d. was so gorgeous! Even trashed in _Trash_ he's gorgeous. Holly Woodlawn is screaming at him "you're a mooch! Mooch! Motherfucker! Why do you have to be unconscious..."

A few things I forgot: motorcycles. (Stage direction: puts hand on hip and adopts mock shocked boy/girl friend voice) "Just exactly what is your *relationship* to those motorcycles??"

Lingis: I've got that book you mention, but haven't read it. But I loved _Abuses_ (if loved is the right word) particularly the stuff about Mexico. I love the way he takes phenomenology to its limits, to its encounter with the universal otherness, or the universality of the encounter with otherness. Such a timely project: to find the limit to 'difference.'

Who's Jelinek?

Straight men: what does anyone see in them?

Straight women: I have this straight girlfriend who wants me to settle down and breed with her. And I tell her, "but honey, you know I'm queer. You know I'm gonna go find some nice boy and take it up the ass." And she says, "that's why I love you." I mean, what do you say to that?
kxx

Date: Thu, 10 Aug 1995 15:15:06 -0700
From: Acker@eworld.com
To: mwark@laurel.ocs.mq.edu.au
Subject: Re: joe delassandro

Oooo can I answer all your questions...First, what are "access issues"? I'm so dumb. It sounds very impressive...Canberra and Dignitaries. My earrings would make too much noise. You must write it up in a book. Now, can I remember everything, I haven't watched Warhol in years. It/he/they were so much part of my early twenties, why I returned to NYC then, they were the first people with whom I identified. Because of Warhol, we were no longer freaks, outside society. It's really partly because of Warhol that I can now get angry when people treat me as an outsider, as in Brisbane that Nicholas Zurbrugg, "tattooed and pierced," because of Warhol (to begin with) I don't even have to think to reply, if you think that, you're the freak. I am society as much as you. Oh, Sylvère. He just makes me so angry. But it's a new day. I slept for ages: I must have worn myself to bits in Sydney (and before). Motorcycles? My relation to motorcycles. Well, I'm a girl. And there's this big hot throbbing thing between my legs, whenever I want/him/her, and he/she's mine and won't reject me like humans have the habit of doing and. It is so cool. To be on/around this thing and there are trees and water all around you, flying through the country, something like freedom. That's the decent side of the American nightmare. If you visit here, come riding. I'm an almost too-safe driver. What I mean by the decent side of the American nightmare: last fall I taught at Univ. of Idaho so I rode out there, what a ride, at times 80 miles of country without a gas station, just me and high yellow plains, and I arrive in what is still the center of the Aryan Nation and here is one of the few places in this country still so wild that bikers don't have to wear helmets. I rode free. You see, dualism's never operative. I don't know about straights. I like guys, but straight guys....? It's like oil and water. I ask them to whip me and they tell me I'm Satan. Straight women are worse. What do I mean by straight? I don't exactly mean "straight" versus "gay." This is where "queer" comes in. It just one of those things everyone I hang with seems to understand. I wouldn't worry about your girlfriend (Sydney girlfriend?) wanting babies. Rainer (that lovely Germ Nazi who almost wrecked my life) taught me something valuable. I used to ask me, "Do you love me?" Well, I asked him once and learned better. He replied, good old journalist that he was, what I feel about you is my business and what you feel about me is your business. Pay attention to your own business. I learned a lot from that one. If you want to get fucked up the ass, go do it. (I'm sure you do.) It's not your problem, is it? Me, straight queer gay whatever and where do nut cakes like me fit in who like getting fistfucked whacked and told what to do?—the only things that appall me are babies. I wonder that anyone is having them in America anymore: childhood abuse is our middle name. Better off like Lingis to find out if there really is someone/something "other." Oh, I'm not being grammatical. Such are the delights of email. I miss you.

Date: ???
From: Acker@eworld.com
To: mwark@laurel.ocs.mq.edu.au
Subject: Re: joe delassandro

All that and I forgot to give you my address. I always miss the space bar. I think that Tracey wrote it on the package, by the way. And I lost her address and I have to send her a delicious thank you. My address: 929 Clayton St., SF, CA 94117 USA phone/fax# (1) (415) 759-6652. The details of identity.

Date: Fri, 11 Aug 1995 10:14:07 +1000 (EST)
From: McKenzie Wark <mwark@laurel.ocs.mq.edu.au>
To: Acker@eworld.com
Subject: Re: joe delassandro

wandering stars
for whom it is reserved
the black names
the dark names
forever
— Portishead

It's too early in the morning to have anything to say. I like this idea of a refusal to be called other. As normal as the next human...Just got a message from Sabina. Her writer's block just burst. Only the chapter on sexuality and women's magazines seems mostly to be about fistfucking, she says. I'm laughing pretty hard about this. Laughing with her, not at her. Something's seized control of the control freak, making the words come out sideways. Don't you love it when that happens?

kxx

Date: Fri, 11 Aug 1995 01:23:01 -0700
From: Acker@eworld.com
To: mwark@laurel.ocs.mq.edu.au
Subject: Re: joe delassandro

Oooo you're more complicated than me. I love it. And you email as much as all of us in SF. I must email RU and Jude (the Saint) twice a day. Life in the wild west. First, you're worried about having babies with one girl and another lover is coming out of the fistfucking closet and there's also an old boyfriend and then, of course, desire. Lord, honey, can you have babies and keep all this going? I slip and slide in a state that resembles the absence in Blanchot's novels. (Not to mention Duras but she's such a romantic, "something" always emerges (relation (too many parentheses to bother with here). Elfriede Jelinek's the name of one of my favorite novelists, Viennese, her new book is _Women As Lovers_. So far simultaneously totally compelling and boring. (First sentence: One day Brigitte decided, that she wanted to be only woman, all woman for a guy, who was called Heinz. She believes, that from now on her weaknesses would be strengths and her strengths very much hidden. Heinz, however, does not see anything endearing in Brigitte, and he finds her weaknesses only repellent. Now Brigitte also takes care of her appearance for Heinz, because if one is a woman, one can no longer turn back from this path, and one must take care of one's appearance. Brigitte hopes that the future will thank her one day by letting her look younger. But perhaps Brigitte doesn't have any future at all. The future depends entirely on Heinz.) and goes on from there, so far with no change. Have started your book. Shit, you're smart. I'm at the edge of being totally awed; if I get in any more awe of you, I won't be able to gossip to you especially about sex and relationships—that always fascinates me most of all. Now I'm writing like Jelinek. Fuck, I'm a style sponge. Was going to see a movie tonight with a friend Lisa and her girlfriend but Lisa just got her lip pierced, sounded like a horrendous piercing, and can't talk. So I watched the new Polanski movie— S>A> post-torture, written by Dorfman. A bit too expected. Should be going over this French translation of an essay—boring. Have been experimenting with what that radio guy showed me—how you can piss and come at the same time—trying to get all my friends here to do it—but I think I'm making myself way over-sensitive. Have to give it up for a day or two.

Date: Fri, 11 Aug 1995 15:02:18 -0700
From: Acker@eworld.com
To: mwark@laurel.ocs.mq.edu.au
Subject: Re: joe delassandro

Oooo real men…one of my favorite subjects. I do know a few only they all have cunts. Last night in my head I made a list of ZOMBIE WOMEN I KNOW (REAL MEN) OR WOMEN I WOULD NEVER COME UP AGAINST. Tracey Moffat was in there. I would never get near offending one of these women and I'll go up against any man. An old friend of mine said I'm the butchest thing he ever met, boy never met me in bed, boy do I switch hard, but then no one is as dictatorial as a masochist, which makes you (as regards your role as public whipping boy, but you're not actually) not so much maso as victim. Or does it? As usual, all the metaphors have started whirling. 'Cause I'm not supposed to be emailing you but buying some books I need, email for early morning, I'm such a schedule slob. Anyhow, back to real men. Down with all metaphors. Does that mean we're on to metonymy? Here I go again. Hmmm, men. It's not an American phenomenon anymore. Wonder why Sabina likes NYC so much. The girls are conservative and the boys are all gay or male feminists or whatever they're called. A non-playful breed. I'll take Nazis any day of the week. Oooo Germs. I forgot about them. They are fun. And trouble. I've got bad taste when it comes to men. And the English. Have to do a few double-flips there, regarding sexual identities, but somewhere in all those codes they're guys. Maybe it's the island mentality. But the coolest thing is someone who can't be gender-identified, total butch girls and boys who go all over the place and smell bad news. Oh well. Never ask me about categories. Real men. I'll introduce you to my motorcycles. I'm not sure what sex they are. Sexy, though. Now sadists are another thing. A good top you can always smell one outside the bed is a really nice guy. No irony. It's how that works. Women, it's different. Boy, are women bitches. Oooo I'm going to get bitchy here. You should have never started me on this topic. No, of course you're not invading privacy—telling me about Sabina. First of all, I don't know her so I'm not trespassing and how could you be trespassing on my territory look what I say to you. And once I start punning, I get worse. By the way, I was only teasing you a little, Ken, about all your lovers— I hope—well, now I'm the one who's apologizing for trespassing. Sometimes email shows its flaws rather clearly. Gaps. Oh, here go the puns. I better get off and get to work. And I was going to ask you about Spinoza. 'Cause I was thinking about ethics last night… finished the Gurdjieff book which was more than fun…and then I dreamed about being a stripper…woke up and dreamed about something else. I don't know if guys can piss and come at the same time. I've never wanted to be a guy but cocks fascinate me—what it's like to have one. Can you piss and come at the same time? Oooo this is like writing? No, I'm going to go to work now…Till later…

Date: Sat, 12 Aug 1995 00:36:19 +1000 (EST)
From: McKenzie Wark <mwark@laurel.ocs.mq.edu.au>
To: Acker@eworld.com
Subject: Re: joe delassandro

Piss and come at the same time? Is this, like, gender specific, or can anybody do it?

Bought a new CD—King Curtis with Nat Adderley and Wyn Kelly. I always come back to jazz…Curtis could really play. A sentimental Gene Ammonds kinda style. Not what you'd expect from his soul stompers.

I've been slagged off in the paper again. Apparently I committed grave ontological errors in a review of Baudrillard. A very senior philostopher (as Zappa usta say) is on my case. How did he know I was a conceptual masochist? I hate pain, but I love the *idea* of suffering. If only I could be _The Nation_'s favourite whipping boy…

Sabina *dreams* of fist fucking, but you'd never get a whole hand in. I know! And it's not that she lacks talented partners. She'd be a dyke, only none of the women she meets have the balls for it. I know, I think I was her girlfriend when we were together. None of which is any secret, so don't think I'm gossiping *too* liberally here.

Miranda, my straight girlfriend, has I think found out I was with you that weekend. And then I went and cancelled our date this week to go to Canberra and meet the prime minister. So she's *very* pissed off. And I couldn't care less. Things would be so much simpler if she didn't love me.

As for Edmund, I haven't called him for weeks. But I should. I think it's finally over, after 13 years. Imagine. Where will I ever find another boy so…talented!

So yes, I guess you could say things are complicated. And that's not counting these two married women I'm flirting with. But I want men! Real men! Where are they hiding?!

(38)

Trying to get my head around Warhol's relationship to money. I think that's the theme for this essay I want to write. I discovered that he started the diary with Pat Hackett as the record of his tax deductible expenses. Perfect! But there is something troubled, quixotic about his relationship with money. It's not that he was neurotic about money (who isn't?) but that he embodies money's neurosis.

And I just wrote a 1000 word response to a review of my book. It was actually quite favourable, but it made me sound like such a routine thinker. I was so angry! I prefer the one where I'm dammed as a pretentious fool.

I think you were in a dream I had this morning, but I don't know what happened in it. All I remember are your eyes.

I don't know who I was when I wrote that book but I'm not that person any more. There's two parts that I can't imagine writing at all. The part about Heidegger and the guy with the shopping bag who stood in front of the tank in Beijing after the shootout in the square. The part about Gorbachev and the theory of representation. I love those bits because they're so nuts, but they were written by some crazed, possessed zombie. I like the way all those black rap stars, usually the really arrogant ones, begin their liner notes by thanking 'the creator' as a thing apart.

Wow! John Garfield is on TV! Now there was a real man…

kxx

Date: Fri, 11 Aug 1995 21:22:32 -0700
From: Acker@eworld.com
To: mwark@laurel.ocs.mq.edu.au
Subject: Re: joe delassandro

That's why Craig was so interesting: (I'm not revealing anything, after all, he's all spread out, in pictures, in girlie mags or whatever they were) when he was fifteen some girl taught him how to stop coming (unless he wanted to). For three months, while pissing, had to stop pissing during the act about ten times. Every time he pissed. Until his muscles were under complete control. I'm sure he doesn't know this, but this is pure Shaivite practice. Like one of the characters in my new book actually being alive. I was so fascinated. So he goes all over sexually 'cause he has no interest in coming. Almost every man I've been with for a long time has been the same way. Not quite so rad as far as the training. I'm fascinated. Now I want to know what women can do. Anyhow, tonight life sucks 'cause Lisa and Karen bowed out again 'cause Karen just had a wisdom teeth pulled, we'll go out drinking later, but I'll never get to see _Bandit Queen_ and _X-Files_ isn't on. Just got email from Ashley [Crawford] telling me to move to Melbourne. If I wasn't such a lazy bitch, I'd do it tomorrow. Girltown is becoming boring. What I intended to write was this long thing, or whatever, about Warhol...I heard all sorts of stories from Malanga about Warhol and money...the guy really had a thing about it, and about collection. He always wore a corset and never had sex—again according to Malanga. But I have to eat and get back to work. So you go for super-fems, eh? My, my. Maybe I'll go over the French translation now. That'll punish me for being bored. I keep thinking that if I get famous enough, I'll be able to get out of here. Thanks for the Spinoza info…though I know you told me all that in Sydney. But I didn't write it down. Imagine trying to correct a French translation of quotes from Judith Butler. Pure punishment. Paying for all my Jewish sins.

Date: Sat, 12 Aug 1995 12:04:25 +1000 (EST)
From: McKenzie Wark <mwark@laurel.ocs.mq.edu.au>
To: Acker@eworld.com
Subject: Re: joe delassandro

Ah yes, Spinoza. I read Michael Hardt's book _Gilles Deleuze: an Apprenticeship in Philosophy_ (Minnesota) and it started to come together for me. Has chapters on Spinoza, Bergson and Nietzsche. Then Deleuze's own book on S. Then the _Ethics_, then _Spinoza and Other Heretics_ by Yirmiyahu Yovel (Princeton). But the _Ethics_ is the thing. The first part is only a few pages and extremely dry. But it's a machine for making the infinite.

Cocks. Yeah, well there have been times when I'd rather not have one. Irigary was right. They take over, they *centralise*. They're like the toys they advertise on TV: less fun than they look.

And they are designed to squirt sperm and then curl up and go home. So to have any real fun, if you have one, involves circumventing these two tendencies, to centralising in space and localising in time.

(41)

You have to find other rhizomes in the nervous system, around this absent centre.

This is why I tend to avoid straight girls—they rarely get it. How boring all this is. To me anyway. With the exception of Miranda. With whom the performance of straightness still seems to me to have some curious edge to it. I guess 'cause she's so 101% femme.

kxx

Date: Sat, 12 Aug 1995 16:17:08 +1000 (EST)
From: McKenzie Wark <mwark@laurel.ocs.mq.edu.au>
To: Acker@eworld.com
Subject: Re: joe delassandro

So what distinguishes a Jewish sin from, say, a Catholic one? Don't quite know where it came from but I think I inherited only one notion of sin: to not follow your 'calling.' I hate the way the word 'vocational' has been so perverted that all it means is 'work.' It's the opposite of work!

I find it curious that Warhol did a money series at the same time as the Campbell's soup series, but nobody made a fuss about it. Perhaps because that was the real scandal. Painting commodities was already old news—all those English portraits of prize dogs and wives and horses, but money…

Yeah, if yr a boy, *not* coming is the most fun you can have. Up to the point where yr whole nervous system is on fire, then it's the only way to come down. Only sometimes I pass out. That used to only happen to me with boys, but lately I've become genuinely versatile.

I've only had one superfemme in life, actually. She had to teach me how to be butch. But unlike the really butch guys she usually hangs out with I've never hit her or tortured her emotionally, and when I got her pregnant I tried to be responsible for that. And I supported her filmmaking ambitions, etc. But I draw the line at giving her all my spare money so she can be a housewife and breed!

Judith Butler in French? What is this thing? Something of yours?

I should go do some work too. I've been in the uni library most of the morning reading back numbers of the _New Yorker_, _Atlantic_, all that. Supposed to be writing something for _Social Text_ about Gingrich and the anti-public sphere. Found this really violent attack on Rupert Murdoch in __The Nation__. It's not that I love Murdoch, but this piece was fucking racist! They wouldn't dare talk about Jewish money the way they talk about Murdoch. It would be obvious how racist and abusive such a line of thought is. But it's like Murdoch is fair game 'cause he's an Australian.

Foreign purveyor of filth and muck invading America: does this sound *familiar*? Owes allegiance to no country, graft and shady deals, contemptuous of civilised values, already got a stranglehold on the UK...I fail to see the difference here between _The Nation_ and Pat Robertson.

There are all these evil Australian characters in American soap opera these days. _Melrose_ has had two. _Models Inc_. _Baywatch_. It's like racism without race. It's OK to hate 'em 'cause they are white. But they are still evil foreigners...

Murdoch, Bob Hughes, Sabina and me: the thing is we all *love* AmeriKKKa. Love it so much we just wanna fuck it up the ass! We can never *be* AmeriKKKa but we can do it in drag! We want Gidget! We want Bob Hope! We want Gilligan! We want Mary Tyler Moore! We want Patty Duke! We want James Brown! We want Dick Van Dyke! We want the Supremes! We want Andy Warhol! We want the Fonz! We want Mamie Van Doren! We want Kathy Acker! We want Liberace! We want Caspar the Friendly Ghost! We want Ice-T! We are your second cousin twice removed come back to claim our inheritance! Gonna eat your soul! Gonna snap crackle your pop! Gonna bomb your bass! Gonna fuck yo' ass! Coz we love you, we love every little ting you do. You made us what we are—your night-mare, your curse...

Whooops, getting carried away here. Slipping into Kierkegaard ...anyway, I can't possibly explain the 'America question' in Australian culture, only there might be something in the idea of an essay on it that comes at it the other way around—the Australia problem in American culture. I mean, we never get any attention! We love from afar.

(44)

Until Murdoch came to town...Um, sorry, thinking out loud.
kxx

Date: Sat, 12 Aug 1995 03:19:04 -0700
From: Acker@eworld.com
To: mwark@laurel.ocs.mq.edu.au
Subject: Re: joe delassandro

Like it when you think out loud. _The Nation_ is getting weird.
Maybe it always was weird. I mean: it looks like the liberals (as _The
Nation_) versus the proles (the militias etc.) with the non-whites
especially the blacks in the middle as fodder—pure war-time. Oh,
I'm not being clear. God knows what you all see in America. I see war
and devastation. The fucking pilgrims leaving England 'cause there
wasn't enough law and rigidity there, coming here hating all ideas,
thought, questioning; the Quakers and the Pilgrims fighting it out
with the money people in NYC and Washington and we're the result.
Great. Don't think just kill 'em all. This country has already been
through its empire and it hasn't even started to think. What I see here
is a big black hole; no wonder everyone's thirsting for religion; thirst
is thirst; they hate the Arabs 'cause the Arabs are cultured. Well, it's
fucking three in the morning and I'm flipping. Will have to get back
to you on Warhol when I'm not flipping. Warhol and money. You
must write about it. Got home drunk and did the French editing (a
catalogue essay for the Pompidou, a huge show on gender, opens in
October, nice little present for me though editing French when

(45)

drunk is …uh…strange…and then burst into tears. Called my friend XY in desperation…why am I flipping out…what the fuck did Australia do to me…XY had no clues and he was/is flipping out worse…he and his wife (they're not actually married, have been together for years and years, have usually had other lovers, are thinking of splitting for a bit, XY just had this affair with a young artist who brought him out of the S/M closet and then she dumped him and he's flipping badly I'm scared he's going to start cutting himself again…so my sobbing seemed minor and not worthwhile in comparison…will have to see XY tomorrow night…he and KY are both great writers…can't figure out why I'm doing this…I haven't acted this way in years…I tour …like…every month and am more than used to the nature of the life…my work's on schedule and…well it's part of a writer's life you just never know if you're about to be homeless or rich…hell, that's usual and I'm more stable economically than I usually am so that can't be it…hating SF?…well I've been doing that for a while and have said that I'll move as soon as I know where and have a job/economic stability…so that's all planned…no reason for this nuttiness there…shit, Ken, it's fucking three in the morning and I'm happily reading about K. Mansfield and instead I'm emailing you as if you're my junk…nearest I ever got to the stuff…I've got to stop this…one email a day…what the fuck is going on?…I don't recognize what I'm feeling or why I'm acting like this…XY said just let it go until it gets so bad that you know what is going on…guess that's good advice…I'm so unused to anything but overwork and lust that I wouldn't recognize a cat if I fell over it…well, just be my friend… maybe this is some weird disease or something and will pass and I'll cool down and be a great normal

(46)

friend...why Australia? I've never thought about Australia beyond having the usual friends who got drunk and ate steak and eggs at five in the morning...(my first intro. to your countrymen)...I'm so fucking retarded no wonder I'm a writer I don't know how to say anything...I like it when you tell me about your relationships 'cause I don't know what one is and someone has to have them...what the fuck is going on with me. I'm sorry, Ken; do be my friend.

Date: Sat, 12 Aug 1995 11:44:20 -0700
From: Acker@eworld.com
To: mwark@laurel.ocs.mq.edu.au
Subject: Re: Subject

Oh let me just apologize for last night's message by explaining America to you. I'm not being pretentious—perhaps here I do find that there are different cultures. Well, overlapping and I'm not you, as they say. (Otherness). Oh Ken. Look, the America you see, for me, isn't the America I live in. The America you see is corporate America and its images. You probably know more about it than me because I don't watch TV. I almost never have, except for movies and the occasional (like) _X-Files_. I wouldn't know a building where some TV show was made from a homeless shelter. As for, for instance, the KATHY ACKER that YOU WANT (as you put it), is another MICKEY MOUSE, you probably know her better than I do. It's media, Ken. It's not me. Like almost all the people I know, and certainly all the people I'm closest to, all of whom are "culture-makers" and

(47)

so-called successful ones, I'm this: part of a culture that doesn't want me. I'm neither scientist/military/doctor/etc. nor fodder and so, I'm no longer on the margins, I'm just being ousted. All of us are and we know it. We're hustling, we're doing the two-step, the dances of those who're historically ousted (i.e. as good-as-dead), because we're trying to survive. Our only survival card is FAME and the other side of the card, the pretty picture, is "homelessness." Poverty exists in England; this is "homelessness." That's who I am; I overwork most of the time; I come up for air (this is the first time in some years that I'm not running five jobs at once, touring and writing a novel and journalism/theory writing and teaching and what other projects like the Mekons' record, and I come up for air and who am I...lonely and scared).

We're rats walking tightropes we never thought existed. No medical insurance; no steady job; etc. This isn't me, Ken, or rather it is me (personal) and it isn't: it's social and political. All my friends are the same. RU copes by doing heroin...XY cuts himself...KY, the most stable, helps XY (their possibly splitting is freaking me)...I...email you. Run to hills that don't exist. My bikes. Let me tell you about the America I live in. It's a war-zone. No wonder I'm fascinated with...by?...your relationships...we have the relationships of too many rats in a cage. No, rats who are hungry. No, rats who don't have maps that work. Looking for maps that work. I'm amazed by your culture: you have maps. Culture. Art. Boring dinner parties. RU isn't walking homeless through the streets. I don't carry a knife to protect. Oh sure, we all look glam while traveling ...we're good at media images...hustlers...this isn't poverty. It's homelessness and

AIDS and a society that's in the process of killing off the middle classes. Fuck the liberals. You want to see "my" country. Get in a car and drive from little town to little town and talk to people. I do it all the time. It's part of touring. I know my students. I know that over half of them come out of serious child abuse, sexual and other. And they don't, by and large, come from poor families. Well, enough. That's my rant, really my apology, of a sort, for my freak-out. I just can't bear seeing the world I live in. I have to hide in overwork. I can't bear seeing what I've become. My friends. I guess when there's no hope, what you do is come and fight. So that's what's happening, who we are. We're fighting the only ways we know how, through culture and no one wants culture, and it's war. The weapons...they're just a form of money...stockpiled...the military still earn more than the doctors. The same damn industry supports the movie industry. That should tell you something.

As for Australia, I guess the Australia of my dreams is not what you'd expect. It started, that Australia for me, a bit, when I had this Australian friend, the steak-and-egg eater, about fifteen years ago. MY phone just rang? Can my phone ring when I'm on this? Weird. It's RU. I'll have to call him back. How can I have two phone lines when I have one? Schizophrenia of machinery? Well, I better get off. I visited all of you, a white culture, sort of split between American and English, funny, a culture that didn't seem to exist though it did, it didn't seem other, but the Australia in my dreams has to do with land. Land and dreaming. I wanted to go there, hit Australia with my bike, pardon the biker terminology, but no time, really seeing Australia for me this time was all interviews and a few days at the end in Sydney making friends. Feel that I never visited Australia. I visited a world I knew that somehow had weird geographical existence and I still have to visit Australia. Does this make sense?

Anyhow, please accept my apology.

Date: Sun, 13 Aug 1995 00:25:56 +1000 (EST)
From: McKenzie Wark <mwark@laurel.ocs.mq.edu.au>
To: Acker@eworld.com
Subject: Re: Subject

Of course I'll be your friend. Am your friend. Write to me about whatever you like. I personally find it very helpful to have friends I can write to about anything and write pretty much daily to a couple of good friends. And now to you. But this is a bit different. A bit special. I don't know the what-why-where of this writing any more than you do, but that's ok. Write me your vertigo, it will be safe with me. I'm spending a lot of time by myself at the moment, so I like to exchange email with you. I'm easing myself into a lazy but consistent writing mode. I think. But why are you crying? What is this precipice from which you don't want to jump?

I'm reading _Pussycat Fever_, speaking of vertigo. Your writing irritates me. Let me quickly add that this is a compliment! Just when I think I've abstracted something from it, found a diagram for it, your reach out from the page and tear it all up. Aphasic phenomenology.

But every now and then some monster makes itself, assembles itself. Those are the bits I especially like.

Just watched Vadim's _Dangerous Liaisons_ 1960. Jeanne Moreau as femme fatale. {Sigh.} Strategy as the only cure for boredom. That was 35 years ago. Now we are bored with boredom. Boredom cubed equals postmodernism.

All I have are diagrams. My love, my power, my wit, my sex—all diagrams.

Ovid's cures for the blues: stay busy; manage one's business affairs; hunting; travel; repetition; misanthropy; the cultivation of other habits; crowds and bustle; art; drinking.
kxx

Date: Sun, 13 Aug 1995 11:40:05 +1000 (EST)
From: McKenzie Wark <mwark@laurel.ocs.mq.edu.au>
To: Acker@eworld.com
Subject: Re: Subject

yes exactly! you take an imaginary map of things 'American' and lay it over another continent like a blanket, and what you have is…The *image* of you is part of that imaginary. Of course I know that's not you; and that's not America. I stayed a bit too long in a restaurant at about 130th St last time I was in NYC. When I stepped

(51)

outside, there was a burning car across the road. I could see the silhouette of a man holding a semi-automatic rifle. I hurried into the subway, tiptoeing over bodies that I assume where sleeping. And so on. But what I'm trying to get at is the irony of *all* of it becoming just a blanket of images. I think everyone in the rest of the world got used to America being a TV show. There can't possibly be real suffering there—it's only a movie. Even if we know that's not so, I think everyone prefers to pretend it's just a movie. Nobody wants to face the fact that the empire is dying. We were basically forced to consume the image of American power; now we consume the image of American violence.

I'm sorry, I shouldn't have started this particular meme and shouldn't have connected you to it. Particularly as I know you were thinking about yr own position, possibilities, futures…So now we've both apologised and we can move on. It pains me that so many good people are not even marginalised any more, they're pushed off the margin. But I have this chronic disease called optimism.

kxx

Date: Sun, 13 Aug 1995 12:07:01 +1000 (EST)
From: McKenzie Wark <mwark@laurel.ocs.mq.edu.au>
To: Acker@eworld.com
Subject: Re: Subject

Ah yes, and your impression of Australia. It isn't quite real either. Altho' it's not a bad image, and it's one Justine and Julian and all of us live in and cling to. I had an insight into this from the other side. I sat in a room with the people who *run* this country, and I realised that they would like to keep this pleasant image together, but they don't know how. All around there is danger. All that is solid melts into air. You should come and do the mad max thing while there's still time. Did I tell you about the Japanese tourists who come here with motorcycles? They ride into the desert and get lost. Some of them die there. The tourist industry doesn't want to talk about it. These people don't realise that there might be no place to get gas and water for a *thousand miles*…Michael Spencer Tjapaltjari died out there. I met him once, very impressive man. His Toyota Landcruiser broke down. They found him dead a week later. Yes the desert is very, very real. Even an experienced bushman can lose his way and die out there. The black fellas had the right idea about the desert. All it's good for is for making epic poetry. Apart from that it should be left alone.…It belongs to the rainbow serpent. There is no 'frontier' in this culture. Just the desert. Death and desert. The black hole of the real at the heart of the sign.

But I digress…what I wanted to say is that I know there's a you there under the rubble of images, and that you is who I'm talking to. The card has two different sides here: on one side is institutionalised cultural authority. That's the card I play. But on the other side is not homelessness for me personally, but the fragility of this whole culture. We all go down with the ship. Ship of empire. The black freighter comes…

kxx

Date: Sun, 13 Aug 1995 13:49:41 -0700
From: Acker@eworld.com
To: mwark@laurel.ocs.mq.edu.au
Subject: Re: Subject

Well, yes. You see that was what was so peculiar for me about "Australia"—I wasn't putting it properly when I last emailed 'cause I was still so freaked. If "your" (said with all irony) America is TV-McDonald's-Madonna, I can't type properly this morning which is about 1:30 PM due to a debauch kind of last night—"Australia" for me was the American-dream-come-true. In your language, ("your," oh irony!) EQUALITY! JUSTICE! REAL SEXUAL RELATIONSHIPS! NICE DINNER PARTIES! FUNDING FOR WRITERS AND OTHER ARTISTS! etc. And I didn't want to come back. Not to here. You see, to maintain the irony, I wanted "YOU" as you want "ME." Usually when I tour, since I've returned from London, it's been through the USA. Then, it's fine to return to SF, for, as far as I know, this is the only place where one can be queer and a woman and do what one wants with full-class citizenship. As if one has that anymore. Coming back from England—that's no fun, but the place is deteriorating so rapidly, "becoming American" and I'm always so—but why?—shocked by how readily the English, especially the Londoners are allowing even liking this, I'm always so in shock from that, that readjustment to America is easier. But this time—I crashed hard. Worse than coke!! You got a bit of the brunt. Sorry. I didn't want to come back to this. But I did. And am. And it's time to work. As you say, time to go on. Thank you for being a sweetie. Virtual geography, as you have said. (Or identity? Shifting in and out?) Last night was RU's birthday, his uncle an ex-big-wig-physicist and now stockbroker was in town and nieces and nephews so I dragged Richard Kadrey (I mentioned him) to the dinner and Bart showed up and Scrappy (all ex-Mondo2000 people) so it was interesting—RU was totally high and smiled through the whole thing and didn't hear a word probably and Richard, being in pins and needles, got super-macho and self-assertive in his pagan way and what was most interesting at the end when we were in this "cyber" bar listening to this SF hippy music, Oh God fucking [Jerry] Garcia's dead and today's the public funeral and the Dead lived in the house opposite to mine, I can't even leave my flat today, every hippy in the world is going to be in front of it, now the papers, always desperate for material, are discussing Leary's about-to-happen death, Leary, as natural, is proclaiming colon cancer "the new thing to explore!," so RU and his uncle are going to go to the Mitchell's Brothers (the local classy sex show) and I want to go and debauch 'cause I need recovery-after-crash but I have to stay with Richard 'cause we still haven't talked and I did drag him to the dinner so I wouldn't have to miss RU's birthday and for some reason all these guys want to sleep with me and I think, well, I should, it would get me over the crash, but I just can't sleep with men. Not with men-men. It's awful all the opportunities I miss. Then, this girl who looks like a boy, her hair all slicked back, a baby dyke walks in and I'm ready to follow her. The only one I can sleep with is RU and that's 'cause he's a girl to me but we have this bad track record, we slept together twice when we first met and the second time he came in me 'cause he has no control and I said, 'cause I'm major-AIDS-phobic, I will never talk to you again until you get tested, and he did and was negative and then we were great friends and then we slept together again twice about a month before I came to Australia and the same goddamn thing happened and he got tested while I was away and is negative so now we're great friends again but I really shouldn't sleep with him 'cause as Jacqueline Suzanne the great prophet said, "Once is enough." God, when I was a kid, my best friend Mel Freilicher and I used to masturbate to Jacqueline Suzanne books. I can't spell today. Oh, daddy. So I remembered a remark you made about Sabina and thought about how I...others?...move through this male-female business, sometimes male, sometimes female, twirling like snakes around each other, that's why it's most interesting. I can't deal with men who don't go both ways. It's too scary. And here's Richard, all freaked and confiding in me, but I can't touch him 'cause he still can't be a girl and men-men freak me. Isn't it all weird? Like when I was with you, I was a guy, you never saw the female part...my psychic said we're like two buddies in the army. It all fascinates me. Well, I got to bed at five and have to do something with today—get the edit to the French guys—which is way late....Thanks again, honey.

Date: Mon, 14 Aug 1995 08:55:10 +1000 (EST)
From: McKenzie Wark <mwark@laurel.ocs.mq.edu.au>
To: Acker@eworld.com
Subject: Re: Subject

well...anytime! Sounds like you're connected to things again. I've been writing—very slowly. But at least getting something done. That and hosing down a little scandal. The story in the weekend paper and it takes a swipe at Sabina without naming her. Sheesh! It's good for

Sabina to realise that these bored suburban husbands who run the media will never accept her. She's passed for straight for a long time and rubbed along and all that, but in the end, if they can't get into her pants they're gonna give her a hard time. I hope she's starting to realise who her friends are in the public sphere.

Mind you, it's true that Sabina has historically fucked whoever has the intellectual skills/contacts she needs at any given moment. But it really is completely uncalculated. She *really* and *actually* desires that which empowers her in the other. Which is what I think men do. So why shouldn't she? There's a great book about it called _Object-Choice_ by Klaus Theweleit. About the wives and lovers of Heidegger, Freud, etc. The idea of women connecting sex to *anything* but romantic love seems to be a big phobia out there. _Basic Instinct_, _Disclosure_, etc.

Men-men. Yeah. I usually feel the same way about women-women! Christ, and these days they're all married! Leave out the straight and married ones and it narrows the field considerably. I'm not so keen on totally gay men either. Purely from the point of view of the problems of social etiquette that then arise. Like my last gay boyfriend who had continually to be told who was gay/straight/whatever so he'd know how to take them. Whereas where I hang out you just don't ask. The way gay culture eliminates ambiguity just really doesn't do anything for me.

Definitely got that feeling of being isolated again. It's why I travel so much. There aren't enough vampires in this town. I mean hey, you've seen it. Here even the *artists* come to dinner and talk about real estate!

kxx

Date: Sun, 13 Aug 1995 17:11:25 -0700
From: Acker@eworld.com
To: mwark@laurel.ocs.mq.edu.au
Subject: Re: Subject

Oh, I know, the straight lesbian world is the most boring of all and they don't like me either. Only place to hang out, the peripheries, and then I refuse to be marginalized (or worse). That's why I'm sick of SF. In a way, this place is a haven…queer meaning "you are normal whatever you do" and there's a sign over the door to SF that reads "straights not wanted here." And I like being a full-class citizen and even having some power in the community. But. There's another sign that reads, in SF, "Boho/Marginal." That I don't like. I don't like prison gates in any form: they make me want to bust out. And I do. I want it all, you know? The legitimacy and the way(s) "I" am. (Do, Imagine, etc.) Sabina's just learning this now? NYC's good: it teaches some hard lessons. Everyone knows about fucking in NYC. But—don't think that it gets anyone anywhere. Everyone fucks. It's the tease that pleases. The playing of the game. They/whoever want/wants to get into her pants? Oh, no. That's far too boring. Maybe, I don't know the situation, but I know my city. My "home."

(58)

They/whoever wants to fuck her. Over and up. Probably because they/whoever wants to be fucked. If she can. And the game starts…NYC's the most damned incestuous place I've ever lived in. Game playing that makes junk-addiction look like baby toys. You can let an emotion out, but you'd better be prepared to have very long media claws. À la Gary Indiana. My favorite old friend. We have yet to see the conclusion of that one. The bits you're saying reminded me of XXXXXX…Lord, I remember going to some Pomo conference Sylvère had a hand in, the early days, and that creep [Bernard Henri] Levy gives a speech (after Sollers has done his usual blather) all about Eve coming out of the rib of Adam and therefore and therefore…So XXXXXX, very beautiful, asks him a question. Then she disappears. An hour or two later, she reappearing, we ask XXXXXX where's she been. "With Levy." "Why?" "Power, baby, power." And XXXXXX went right for it. From BH Levy through The X-Files, going straight or gay according to the power-lines, should I say "the power-brokers"?, until she hit Hollywood and XXXX XXXXXXXXX. Oh, the tales we don't tell. (Am I spelling X.X.'s name correctly?) The damn problem with email is that now I can't see your letter. I remember there were other things I wanted to say/reply to. Oooo, what a lazy day. I've given up on it. Sunday. Am preoccupied by Katherine Mansfield—Bloomsbury meets D. H. Lawrence. I must be going weird. I've started writing too, thank God, doing a male voice this time, all-male adventures. Feels good. Got a female voice in the background, Cassandra. (I do voices, schizoid that I am. Or paranoid? Or whatever…Fucking Freudians…) Need groceries first. Wanted to send you first two chapters of new novel 'cause you might be amused but can't figure out how to send files on this thing/mind/whatever it is. Save Mansfield for the early morning when I'm too tired to do anything else. Ashley just mentioned Sabina in an email. I should meet her, said A. I told him to talk to you. Glad you're writing again—there's the ground (for me, certainly, for you?). Bye for today…

Date: Mon, 14 Aug 1995 12:05:59 +1000 (EST)
From: McKenzie Wark <mwark@laurel.ocs.mq.edu.au>
To: Acker@eworld.com
Subject: Re: Subject

Sydney is a pretty queer town too, but if anything that's now part of the problem. The gay/lesbian power centres have realised they have power and are using it to exclude, thus making them feel more powerful. I have to say something about it at QueerLit this year without alienating too many of the people I like there, who are mostly old-time faggot writers. The survivors. I really couldn't bring myself to give them a hard time. We're lucky they're still around.

Sabina only really came out a few years ago. And at 34, people are no longer putting her in the box labeled 'will settle down soon.' Whereas nobody ever had those kind of illusions about me. So I guess I'm her recruitment agent for the bad life!

Gotta do some more effective networking in this town, is what all this is putting me in the mind to do. I'm in danger of getting a bit isolated. And this thing in the weekend paper is making me feel like I'm a bit vulnerable, and so are a lot of my friends. Not really sure of the backing of either the mainstream or the marginal media.

kxx

Date: Mon, 14 Aug 1995 15:28:05 +1000 (EST)
From: McKenzie Wark <mwark@laurel.ocs.mq.edu.au>
To: Acker@eworld.com
Subject: Re: Subject

Got interrupted. Great story about XXXXXX. She directed that zombie apocalypse movie, right? Not so keen on the space cop movie or the gay bank robber movie.

By all means send me the chapters, if you figure out how. I'd love to read them. I've never read Mansfield or Lawrence. What am I missing out on?

The penny finally dropped for me about something: Sabina uses sex for advancement—but the way a man would. Unconsciously. Desire to become something else. It's not desire as lack, but desire as production. That's what people don't expect and don't get. I kind of admire that, actually. But enough about her. Lets talk about me! I've never been able to 'use' sex for anything. Could never quite see it as part of a strategy. So I'm fascinated by people who use it one way or another. I don't have any moral objection. I know I've been used. But I knew I was being used, so I don't see that I have any right to complain. If anything, I was taking advantage of the fact that I was being used! Now wouldn't that be even more reprehensible?

The thing that really bores me is the people who think that in exchange for the odd fuck I'll do their homework for them. Sure, like I'm gonna explain Baudrillard to some fresher in exchange for getting fresh. (Interesting expression that: does it exist in American? to 'get fresh' with someone…) But the old sex/knowledge economy is really under attack here. So now the students complain that uni is too impersonal. Again I don't have any moral objection—just not interested.

Not sure what I *am* interested in at the moment, which is a bit of a worry!
kxx

Date: Mon, 14 Aug 1995 00:12:38 -0700
From: Acker@eworld.com
To: mwark@laurel.ocs.mq.edu.au
Subject: Re: Subject

Oooh, are you really freaking out about what the media says? I mean, do a Julie Burchill and regard them as looking for a good bitch-fight? Lord, if I got ragged from what the media says about me, though I always do, I'd have suicided, though that's not a proper word, long ago. Did I ever tell you this story...When _Empire Of The Senseless_ came out in England, front page of the literary part of _The Independent_ ran something like ACKER JUNKY. So I'm at the Groucho that night (my club) with my friend Neil [Gaiman] and Neil knows the guy who wrote the piece, he's sitting at a near-by table, so Neil says he's going to go over and say hello, do I want to say anything. Brat by birth that I am, I say, of course not. Rethink and say to Neil, oh ask him if he wants to buy any drugs. Neil leaves, returns, tells me the guy (who's a hulking six-footer) is scared that I'm going to beat him up. I mumble something, like my weight and height. Neil replies, Oh he knows you're a body-builder. Some junky, eh? God bless the media. But you are part of the crew, aren't you? Oh me too. It's all slip and slide. RU sometimes yells at me that I take things too seriously. So now I can yell at you. As for loneliness...I'm going to read your other email...

Date: Mon, 14 Aug 1995 00:46:51 -0700
From: Acker@eworld.com
To: mwark@laurel.ocs.mq.edu.au
Subject: Re: Subject

Huh, what does "I *am* interested in at the moment" mean? Sex? If you haven't noticed from the last email, I'm dead drunk. Not quite dead, yet. But drunk. Have been working on that goddamn French edit since 5:00, shit. It's twelve thirty. (12:30 am) Just have to print it out and fax it. Then I can watch _Camille Claudel_, the rest of. Have been bribing myself. So what aren't you interested in? Let's talk about you? (says me with pure drunken gumption). Usually I'm scared of intruding and don't say, what the hell's going on? I mean, sex for advancement? I just never thought it worked. What do people get from other people? I just never thought much. The odd cuddle. I don't know. And then...everything. But we're not talking about that. (I'm about, drunkenly, to slip into Bataille and Blanchot, my favorite old shoes). You sound in a funny mood, sweetie. I don't think I've ever gotten a gig through sex and I've certainly lost quite a few. Like...as I was telling RU...I could have become a lesbian star in Australia but instead I go around fucking guys. Of course, says RU, you always fuck up through sex. I mean, looking good and flirting and all that shit—yeah that does good...I'm trying to be cynical here about sex...oh I'm too drunk. And good sex is so rare and so fabulous and wonderful...who would want to spoil it by fucky career and all that shit that bores. I'm as ambitious as the next guy but enough is enough...working till midnight...that's what gets the old career moving...just fucking working your ass off. I guess knowing the right people does it too, though that can be a bore, but the minute you get sexually involved with someone, you get involved with trouble and that can backfire. Usually does. Unless you've got some real caring involved. So I don't know about this fucking for career. For about a year no it was more I slept with some of my female students 'cause I don't know it's easy it was...like eating candy when you want a full meal. But...candy's not so bad. I just don't know, Ken. I'm no one to ask...my life's solitude and mess. Now, solitude...I was going to yap on 'cause I know about that...It's real rare to have someone to talk to. I guess that's what I think about all this fucking around. Usually you can talk to X about this…like I can't talk to RU about anything I read or write 'cause he hates books and theory…but I can hang with him…and I can't have fun with Richard the way I do with RU…and it goes on and on, it's really rare, I think in terms of territory, that there's immense territory with a person. It's so cool when there is. Like, freedom. Maybe, I'm thinking this way 'cause I've sort of reached a stage in my career when I can start, I think, calling a few shots, saying I'm going to work in these ways, with friends, I want friendship to be involved, this new book and record for important is important 'cause this is the first time I've done it this way. And the CD-Rom game with Artemis. All through friends, kind of my way. I say, kind of 'cause I always have to play ball with the business guys. But I don't want to ass-lick Pantheon and William Morris anymore. I don't think I have to. By ass-lick I don't mean sex. Honestly, I don't think that one was to be that simplistically cynical. Oooo I don't mean it that way (that's harsh). Of course, it's who knows who. Well, I'm rambling drunkenly. As for friends— it's what I've got. I'm all into networking even though I have a propensity, which is sneaking up on me again 'cause I want to write, delve down, to isolate myself. But I'm blabbing about myself. We're supposed to be talking about you. But I'm learning. I bet students want to sleep with you 'cause you're gorgeous and they're into a bit of worship moving into transference. That's what I usually get, with or without sex, transference. Quite a problem. Which brings me to [Klaus] Theweleit. He's a friend of Larry Rickels, I met him last year when I was teaching at UCBS. Big old kind of hippy, psychiatrist wife and two hulking sons. I gave them my apartment. A sweetheart and bit of a nut case…did a surprisingly nineteenth century talk on [Elias] Canetti. Whose writing I love. I've wanted to read his new book for a while…have only read extracts. Will have to phone Larry. I can't spell anymore. Oh, have to get back to work and make the French happy. Monsieur, voulez trouver dans ce lettre un…blahblah-blah. Oh I'm sorry, I'm being goofy. Maybe I'll get rich and then I can be goofy all my life. It turns out that most of my long-term lovers were power-brokers and actually rich and half the time I was so dumb I didn't know it…I only found out that Sylvère has lots of money after he left me and got married. I always wondered why he was buying all this property…And Rudi used to wave hundred dollar stacks in front of my face and boast 'cause he was buying me a falaf…I can't spell it…fuck red wine…sandwich. As for Melissa, oh that girl…I got in trouble there…way over my head…she's married now with children…it wasn't serious for her but I kind of started making speeches for her dad and I think that's what got me into trouble in England. I don't know. The English don't come clean about these things. That's the real game, politics. I found out and lost the only place I ever sort of regarded as home. Oh well. Best to stay in one's garden but Voltaire was a boring writer and sex is one of the greatest things there is. I better get off I'm so drunk…

Date: Mon, 14 Aug 1995 21:33:54 +1000 (EST)
From: McKenzie Wark <mwark@laurel.ocs.mq.edu.au>
To: Acker@eworld.com
Subject: Re: Subject

Oh, I don't care what the media says in the sense of feeling personally wounded or offended or anything. I care in the sense that there is a war on! The information war, as old Bill Lee used to say. It's also an experiment. Media is my obsession, see, and it's an ongoing aesthetic experiment. I'm an artist and my chosen materials are the media. So there's a politics and an aesthetics. And a fascination. I'm trying to get beyond Debord and Baudrillard…I'm a leftwing columnist (a fifth columnist!) in a Murdoch paper, see, and one of my former editors and a 'mate' as one says in the vernacular, a buddy, has turned against someone I'm closely identified with in public life…Hence all the activity around this. It brings out the Stalinist in me. What you call liberalism still exists here. But the neo-cons are coming…and as in the US one of their chosen battle-grounds is the media.

k

Date: Mon, 14 Aug 1995 21:39:21 +1000 (EST)
From: McKenzie Wark <mwark@laurel.ocs.mq.edu.au>
To: Acker@eworld.com
Subject: Re: Subject

…but I loved that ACKER JUNKY story! There really are some scumbags in the media. Once you realise you're dealing with a scumbag then it's just a question of figuring out how to manipulate them or fuck with them or go around them. This guy I think we're gonna fuck with. I did warn you I had a Stalinist streak didn't I?…You

(67)

know what message I would have sent to that asshole who wrote the ACKER JUNKY story? "I'm holding for you. Meet me out the back in 10 minutes, or I'll have to hand it over right here in the club." Then you fold up a little bit of paper...

kxx

Date: Mon, 14 Aug 1995 22:53:33 +1000 (EST)
From: McKenzie Wark <mwark@laurel.ocs.mq.edu.au>
To: Acker@eworld.com
Subject: Re: Subject

well it was a pretty fabulous drunken rave, I gotta tell you!

Yeah, sex has nothing to do with work for me. Work is just work, alone with the keyboard, and speaking in public—my advertising. I'm very comfortable talking to a crowd. I just sold myself in public for 15 years. It's better than sex—sometimes!

I like the way "let's talk about me" always slides into "talk about you" and vice versa. What would Blanchot say about that? I've not read much Blanchot, incidentally. Where should I start?

Theweleit lecturing on Canetti? I adore Canetti. I was struggling with the sheer compacted beauty of _Crowds and Power_ when I wrote my China chapters in the book. But it's those notebooks that

(68)

really get to me. It's like Canetti found the still, dead, quiet centre that was the tornado of the 20th century.

This gorgeous woman I've been flirting with just appeared on my TV. I invited her to that _21*C_ magazine launch you did, and she came, but she had to meet her husband so she made her excuses and left. I gave her exquisite, tiny hand a squeeze as she left and it was shaking. Now, the thing is, I don't even really want to have sex with her or anything. Sometimes the flirting is as good as it gets. The sheer unlimited possibility of it…

Shit!…you are on TV. Yes you. Right now. Spooky. I miss you. It's a good piece. Just you talking and you reading. You give good sound bite honey, as if you didn't already know…

But let's talk about me. A brief sexual history:

17, Glen. Aboriginal guy. Linguist. Last person alive who speaks his people's language. His love for me wasn't legal, and wasn't really reciprocated.

19, Edmund. I lived with him. Big mistake. This is the story of this bottom learning how to top. Now he's my emotional dependent.

22, Helen. Schizophrenia. Wild, scary ride. She's dead now and I miss her greatly. I keep her picture where I can see it every day.

27, Miranda. I was no. 6 on her string, and I made my way to number 1, and then it was no fun anymore.

31, Noel. Big art bureaucrat. I was treated as his girlfriend wherever we went, which is to say, patronised and ignored. My feminism!

32, Sabina. Infinite territory. Too scary to last. She needs a wife, and I'd almost be that for her, only she quickly comes to despise anyone who doesn't rise to her challenge.

They are the secret characters in all my essays and the book. Only I know where the bodies are hiding in the text.

Territory you said. That's the thing. With whom does one share which territory, and how do they intersect? The one way streets cut through me—they have those names on them. But there's not much territory to speak of any more. I've been careless. Lost too many friends. Or did they lose me?

kxx

Date: Mon, 14 Aug 1995 10:51:25 -0700
From: Acker@eworld.com
To: mwark@laurel.ocs.mq.edu.au
Subject: Re: Subject

Oh I have all these replies but can't do it now 'cause I have to get to the acupuncturist so he can clean up my drunken liver so I can go out, or stay in, and do it again. Was going to tell you that all night, well, when I wasn't asleep, I was feeling badly about that xxxxx story, that you might have thought that I was talking about your and Sabina's relationship. I wasn't...I was just slipping, as usual, on a remark you had made...my memory playing. I get brutal...it's my fucking Aries blundering over-energy. And then I woke up this morning, remembering how I woke up with your hands around my head, how rare that is, usually in few-night-stands people perfunctorily (wrong spelling) embrace and roll away from each other, hands on my head, around, that exquisiteness of caring, and if I got that from just a three-night stand, what must there be between you and Sabina? I felt...oh...I've blundered...my silly xxxxx story. Old goat tearing up the ground again. But your email has put my head somewhere still. Still, honey, I'll try not to blunder again. And shall reply to your emails later. After movie tonight. Now to the acupuncturist to pay non- Catholic penances for all my recent sins (red ones, of course, oh wine!) I miss you too

---

Date: Mon, 14 Aug 1995 18:46:43 -0700
From: Acker@eworld.com
To: mwark@laurel.ocs.mq.edu.au
Subject: Re: Subject

I get it. Wait...I have to get to your next email...

Date: Mon, 14 Aug 1995 18:47:27 -0700
From: Acker@eworld.com
To: mwark@laurel.ocs.mq.edu.au
Subject: Re: Subject

Do you? Now I've got to your next email so I can ask you lots of questions...Oh I can't help it...this fucking Mekons record....Like Sally's singing I've got a dream I've got a dream...all just beautiful and then you hear...not exactly background...and all the rich men begin to die. Now they're singing Antigone went wild 'cause Oedipus was blind. But it's not arty. It's hot. Oh I'm dying of happiness. I'm never having a book that isn't sung again. Now, Antigone goes wild 'cause Oedipus is blind my cunt come out may my cunt be wild...oh I'm gonna die...but I promise...I shan't mention it again...me, narcissist...it's just that I just got it in the mail...Touch-And-Go the record company are really happy and flying me to Chicago to finish it off and we'll tour in the winter—shit it's just my American part all I ever had in this country was wildness and rock-n-roll...now, no more I promise...the real reply (next) is your time

Date: Mon, 14 Aug 1995 18:47:45 -0700
From: Acker@eworld.com
To: mwark@laurel.ocs.mq.edu.au
Subject: Re: Subject

OK—and I approve of that Stalinism…I'm the sneaky sort who sidles up to you and sticks the knife in when you're not looking…I wait for my time, so to speak…one pirate style…but I agree. So give it to the bugger. But explain more to me. How are the sides lining up? And how does the US media link in? I'm fascinated by this stuff. Excuse all the pirate references…I just got the rough cut of the songs for the Mekons and my record/CD and I'm going nuts on pirates. There are two songs that are so fucking gorgeous…oh well this is your time…I'll tell you about them later…

Date: Mon, 14 Aug 1995 19:01:26 -0700
From: Acker@eworld.com
To: mwark@laurel.ocs.mq.edu.au
Subject: Re: Subject

OK here I am again. Final reply. For now. You asked for it. You see, I can't talk about you, or haven't so much, well I am a big old narcissist or selfish or whatever… but mainly 'cause I've been shy about trespassing on territory. Lived too many years in England. Didn't want to bug you…you know I've been working hard for your friendship, Ken, and am still a little scared that you won't want to be my friend. But, you asked for it. I have about a hundred cats living in me and all of them are curious. So in order to talk about you, I get to ask questions.

1. The last night we slept together, why didn't you want to touch me? (You don't have to answer this one. I've thought of all sorts of possible

answers and they run the gamut from understandable even cool to awful. But you do have to answer the next question.)

2. How should I have acted? I fucking didn't know. Ignored you? Held you? I didn't have a clue and I was scared to do the wrong thing.

Now, more general questions. I want to know everything. DETAILS. I love details and as I said, I'm curious. Like gay men send each other, via email, Matias showed me this, all these statistics, but they're boring statistics (size of cock, as if that matters. Unless someone's frightfully small or large, who cares. Cocks grow and shrink according to emotion. And it's how they're used. Or not. Anyhow.) So, details.

1. What do you like best sexually? This has to be...hot memories. 'Cause who knows what the future bears and sexuality's always changing...Details, please.

2. What turns you on in women when you're in bed with one? And what doesn't? I know these all involve emotional answers, for the mind/body duality's for shit so I guess I don't expect you to answer...but...what the hell. I can try.

3. I should ask about guys, but at the moment I'm not so curious. But I want to know about blow-jobs. How to give the best blow-jobs? Guys are good at that.

I've got more questions, but there's or here's a start. Re flirting. I fucking love chasing after someone, too, I learned to in England; in the United States pre-AIDS it used to be that if you didn't sleep with someone before you knew his name, you weren't going to. Women a bit different. And, likewise, actually for me a lot of the time, I didn't really want to sleep with the person once I get him/her. But I can't talk about myself. Those are the rules now. And I'm good. So you have to tell me all the details of what turns you on...i.e. what has turned you on (that's how memory works, oh shit a discourse on time). Re Blanchot: Blanchot has a little book in which there's an essay on Bataille and one on Duras. The one on Duras is kind of patriarchal...the one of Bataille is where he goes into this sort of schemata about self and other. It's totally cool. I can repeat it to you if you want...I use it a lot...don't want to bore ...OK...Bye-bye (Oooh I wanted to ask you about power too. Like with Sabina...how the power-sex spirals worked. Well, next time.) You'll probably hate me after all these questions anyway. At least, you won't mind me blabbing so much about myself.

Date: Tue, 15 Aug 1995 10:26:55 +1000 (EST)
From: McKenzie Wark <mwark@laurel.ocs.mq.edu.au>
To: Acker@eworld.com
Subject: Re: Subject

Hey it's all right. Hey it's all right. The XXXXXX story was apropos. I think it's a rarer kind of behaviour than people imagine. Mostly motives are messy. Sabina really thinks she desires whomever it is who is *useful* to her at that moment. Which I think is more of a butch thing to do. It comes from constructing a self in motion in the world that proves it exists to itself thru achieving things. Miranda was another story—classic femme thing about sexual power. Her only form of power.

Fiona Giles, who's the editor of the _Dick for a Day_ volume, wants me to write about the homme fatale—so this is a subject I've been thinking about anyway. I think I've got the _Dick for a Day_ story done, too. Trying to write pretty conventional pornographic story, but with a melancholy tone. It's not exactly art, but it's fun!

…it's the lying half awake, in the morning with someone, that I like best. Like happy mammals.

kxx

Date: Tue, 15 Aug 1995 14:00:19 +1000 (EST)
From: McKenzie Wark <mwark@laurel.ocs.mq.edu.au>
To: Acker@eworld.com
Subject: Re: Subject

Well I'm delighted to hear that the Mekons thang makes you happy! I wanna hear it right now!

kxx

Date: Tue, 15 Aug 1995 14:06:55 +1000 (EST)
From: McKenzie Wark <mwark@laurel.ocs.mq.edu.au>
To: Acker@eworld.com
Subject: Re: Subject

There are various channels here thru which the old cold war right tries to get ameriKKKan neo-con stuff to fly. Like 'political correctness.' In Australia, left wing folks used to joke about being a bit too 'ideologically sound.' But 'politically correct' has beat out the local expression 'ideologically sound'—thanks to press beat ups on PC. There was an attempt to get the culture wars going, but it didn't fly. Liberal common sense is still, thankfully, liberal common sense. Some of the more prominent 60s and 70s public leftwing intellectuals have moved right 'cause they're alienated and disenfranchised by the whole theory thing. That's a tricky one for people like me 'cause one doesn't want to alienate them further. On the other hand we wanna bury them and take their slots in the public sphere. It's an oedipal thing. Gotta kill mom 'n pop to make some space...and they know it. Ironically, the main problem here is that the old new left is *too* strong in the public sphere.

kxx

Date: Tue, 15 Aug 1995 14:39:00 +1000 (EST)
From: McKenzie Wark <mwark@laurel.ocs.mq.edu.au>
To: Acker@eworld.com
Subject: Re: Subject

Lemme clear up some stuff first.

1. our last night together. We weren't together enough for you to notice the pattern, but what tends to happen with me is that I have to curl up in a ball by myself in order to get to sleep, but I wake up in the morning all wrapped around you. I don't know why this happens, but it always happens. So that thing where I kinda withdraw into myself and into my own space in the bed—I'm really sorry about that. I know it looks bad, but there's nothing I can do about it. When I need to sleep it's the only way I can get to sleep, but somehow when I *am* asleep I get friendly again. I really liked sleeping with you. Really.

2. uh, I think I just answered question 2 in there.

3. blow job theory. I don't think there's much more you need to know! I don't always come when I'm sucked, but I love it anyway. Precisely because it isn't a climactic kinda thing. And sometimes when I do come I come close to passing out, and that isn't always so pleasant so sometimes I back off, come back down to a plateau without going over the top. I'm not often very dick-centered these days when I get horny. I had this really strong urge to fuck you a couple of times, but the condoms were in my jacket where they always are and I didn't want to, like, break the spell and negotiate all that. It seemed more interesting to me to keep doing what we were doing. I was mostly feeling pretty voluptuous, lazy, but also a bit devotional. You were adorable—and I mean that in the strict sense, not the vaguely superlative sense. I wanted to adore you by making you

(78)

come. I get pretty involved in that. It's where things merge to form one singularity. I think it was the second time that you sucked me off and I was feeling totally voluptuous, very narcissistic, the body lost to itself. I wasn't sure if I should let go, 'cause when I did I nearly blacked out. It was very affirming for me. On the last night we slept together I really wasn't feeling very well, I realised, so I got you to massage my back and neck. A compound hangover! When I'm not feeling well I have a bad habit of trying to hide it. I had this feeling that you were picking up bad signs but not realising that it was just because I wasn't so well, but it was a bit beyond me to explain or anything at that point. And the morning after was like—shock! What now?!

But that's OK. I feel like I'm working pretty hard on being yr friend too, by the way. I feel like I've been chattering away, just establishing a channel with you. But now I'm comfortable with there being a channel, so I don't mind talking about whatever. It's like getting the rhythm to a waltz right. Only who's gonna lead? Does it always work that way? Is there always a butch/femme moment in every exchange? That's my theory, anyway. I always maintain that there's no escape from the b/f dialectic, but that anyone can occupy either pole if they know how, and that it can oscillate wildly if you let it/ want it. I don't believe in the androgyne or the bisexual as the middle. If it looks that way it's because it's oscillating too fast for the eye to see/hand to feel...

kxx

Date: Tue, 15 Aug 1995 14:42:25 +1000 (EST)
From: McKenzie Wark <mwark@laurel.ocs.mq.edu.au>
To: Acker@eworld.com
Subject: Re: Subject

I'll save the Ken/Sabina story for another time. It's not that I'm reluctant to talk about it, just that you n me is a more interesting story for the moment!

And do explain Blanchot to me sometime. It won't bore me at all—I love theories! I'm working on a quite different approach, the Spinoza-Deleuze axis at the moment. But I would like to know how Blanchot fits in to all of the other French appropriations of Hegel's master/slave dialectic of recognition, which seems to me to be where Bataille comes from...

kxx   .

Date: Tue, 15 Aug 1995 00:43:39 -0700
From: Acker@eworld.com
To: mwark@laurel.ocs.mq.edu.au
Subject: Re: Subject

Oh I always thought androgyny, apart from the literal meaning, meant "all over the place," "oscillating back forth up down, etc." Kind of. What an awful definition. Anyhow, I never thought of "bisexual" as "in the middle." Though I could see how some hard-core lesbians could take it that way. Like…you can't decide, girl, can you? Anyhow…I guess I think of bi, though I hate the word though I don't know why, as sleeping with both sexes. But. But but but but. I just saw this amazing film _Bandit Queen_ which I've been trying to see for a week now and now I have to find out all that happens with women not just in white European countries. As if there's a "white" anymore (yeah fucking!) (But that's another argument.) Anyhow, this film is the first real stuff I've seen about women in India and besides that it's cool. And I thought, toward the end, whoever I end up sleeping with, male female no one etc., I'm always going to be dyke-identified. It's political, 'cause I've gone through so much and women have and do go through so much shit and often don't emerge. And and. I'm being sentimental. And men go through it too. But not. (I'm trying to avoid thinking dualistically here.) Anyhow, to avoid the loops of the mind, what does that say about "bi"? I mean, it was good to go out with my girlfriends and see this film and sit with my legs all spread and sit before the movie in the bar talking about piercing and coming while pissing and whatever else and watch the two old guys stare in some sort of strong emotion, like we were wiping our cunts all over the floor, I felt, it's our turn now to do that, wipe cunt, and I don't ever want to lose that. "Bi" just doesn't hold. The word. But all this has to be negotiated with the reality of people, friends, who my friends and lovers really are (dare I use the word "lovers"…it's been so long…I'll have to give you my rotten minimal love history sometime…). Anyhow, thanks for your answers: you cut right to my angst and answered directly and gently. So I guess now we've

(81)

gone through the shit and I can just blab to you. I'm awful at making sense. Talked to Fiona Giles today about the story, I want to do it 'cause I'm writing all this male-male stuff (sex) at the moment. For some reason vulnerability is lying there for me, I'm trying to find out about vulnerability, do it, go there, 'cause my psychics keep telling me I'm the closed clam of the years and no one can get in. Well, my psychics don't have to tell me this it's so fucking obvious. Anyhow, for some reason vulnerability lies in the male-male. Isn't that weird. I'll never understand why I write what I do/as I do. Now explain the neo-cons to me—i.e. Australian version. How do they relate to the American lot?

Date: Tue, 15 Aug 1995 00:56:55 -0700
From: Acker@eworld.com
To: mwark@laurel.ocs.mq.edu.au
Subject: Re: Subject

Oooh I forgot the butch/femme thing. Now explain it to me. The way a lot of girls I know see it: there's butch/femme and then there's top/bottom. You can be a top femme and a butch bottom. A lot are. And then there are those, sometimes, me who can't figure out butch and femme. Top and bottom of course is clearer. Is it just fashion? 'cause everyone switches. Sometimes I think I know and then I try to figure out what I am, I always say different things, 'cause I don't know. I know I'm awful at topping in bed. I look at a girl who wants it and feel inadequate. But I can do it if I really care—it's

(82)

easier for me with a guy. But then, I'm very demanding. I think. I don't know how one judges oneself. By the other's judgment? Or lack of understanding (as Blanchot puts it)? Oh, I agree with you re power: someone's always taking the lead, but I think it gets real complicated once you're more than surfacely …I forget the word…like enacting with someone. I guess it's easier, I find it so, when on the surface there's a split between top and bottom. 'cause all this stuff about equality not only stinks but makes life very difficult and actually masks some ugly possibilities for violence. But it's a play. Oh well. I'm repeating myself. And you have to explain what you mean, 'cause maybe we're thinking of different things. Like…when we email… forgetting all my narcissism…is that the right word?…who's taking the lead? I know that when we were face-to-face I was into hearing you talk, but that was because I was bloody fascinated. But I can't do that with email…I guess I could but then it would only be one-sentence emails and that doesn't feel like enough contact.

Date: Tue, 15 Aug 1995 21:52:05 +1000 (EST)
From: McKenzie Wark <mwark@laurel.ocs.mq.edu.au>
To: Acker@eworld.com
Subject: Re: Subject

I had a bit of an insight into otherness through Miranda's family. Her father is the grandson of the last Maharaja of Kerala, the southern Indian state now run by the communists. Anyway, the old ruling class was matrilineal and to some extent matrilocal and matriarchal. So the way everything works is really different and completely unexpected. The really bad part is the racism—because Miranda's mother is white she's a nobody. Whites are just barbarians. The men held the symbolic office (Maharaja, or great prince) but the women controlled the property! This is in the far south, where the influence of Islam is extremely weak and where the caste system isn't so elaborate.

kxx

Date: Tue, 15 Aug 1995 22:00:31 +1000 (EST)
From: McKenzie Wark <mwark@laurel.ocs.mq.edu.au>
To: Acker@eworld.com
Subject: neo-cons

The neo-con movement is really weak here. There's very little on the religious right that has much influence, except in the 'outback.' The old conservatives have lost ground with the end of the cold war. They've outlived their usefulness. But that doesn't stop them importing all of the American tactics, or trying to.

The real problems are on the left! The old new left is well entrenched in the media and the bureaucracies, but it's getting pretty reactionary, out of touch, self-interested. The left of the Labor party is in favour of stricter censorship, etc. They're a real worry! So it's a question of shifting alliances, etc. And there hasn't been anything like the

Vietnam war or the Reagan offensive to bring people together. The networks aren't there. We're very vulnerable.

kxx

Date: Tue, 15 Aug 1995 22:03:36 +1000 (EST)
From: McKenzie Wark <mwark@laurel.ocs.mq.edu.au>
To: Acker@eworld.com
Subject: queer as fuck / fuck as queer

Yeah, I always 'identify' with the 'gay and lesbian community,' express my solidarity' with them—so they have to do the same in return! What do they think, I'm gonna get *half* queer bashed 'cause I'm *half* gay?!

kxx

Date: Tue, 15 Aug 1995 22:17:03 +1000 (EST)
From: McKenzie Wark <mwark@laurel.ocs.mq.edu.au>
To: Acker@eworld.com
Subject: love's executioner

What does Baudelaire say: the lovers come face to face, eye to eye, and in an instant one blinks, and in that instant it is decided: who shall be loves victim, and who love's executioner.

(85)

Yes, 'equality' in the sense of the double, the exact equal, is a myth. So the ethical question is: how can difference remain fluid, open? Or: which top/bottom relations are *justified*? (The word hierarchy comes from hieros—the sacred, which is what justifies what is justified).

Butch/femme and top/bottom seem to me to be different articulations of the same thing: the incommensurable relation, the coming together of things that are not the same, in a relation than then makes of that assemblage something also singular. I can see now that I've tended to make the gender polarity pretty absolute, but it's just an actualisation of one of many possible (virtual) forms of the fundamental relation, which is difference. The mistake is to make a fetish of *what* differentiation produces: gay/straight; butch/femme; top/bottom, etc. Whenever these get hardened into something 'natural,' into the law, I get suspicious.

Even when our friends do it: the gay community, etc.

(When I think this, I realise I cannot have a home. There's no bound within which this thought can call itself at home. anti-Heidegger...shit! I just realised what the 'New York chapter' of my next book is about...)

kxx

Date: Tue, 15 Aug 1995 11:06:02 -0700
From: Acker@eworld.com
To: mwark@laurel.ocs.mq.edu.au
Subject: Re: Subject

OK, endless crap on Blanchot coming...but after I've had breakfast. I'm too hungry a monster to do anything else. Just been doing agent-wants stuff prior to desired FOOD. And...an invitation: if you are going to come through SF, on your way to Montreal—which I would love—may I offer one flat, either my bed or a small study with a futon in it, (I have a two bedroom which is actually one large room with sliding doors in the middle and a small study off the hall, and the usual kitchen and bathrooms all covered in books and computer crap), and if you tell me when you're coming and what you enjoy, arrangements to meet whoever you want to meet, tickets to performance art (we don't call it that here...there's a SOLO MIO festival in September, for instance, with Eric Bogosian, I forget who else, no breakfast, and I know the producers 'cause they want me next year), theatre, opera, whatever, or else a set of keys and you do as you please to your heart's content. As you like it—the only policy. You were good to me in Sydney and I would like to respond (and, of course, see you again)

Date: Tue, 15 Aug 1995 17:05:49 -0700
From: Acker@eworld.com
To: mwark@laurel.ocs.mq.edu.au
Subject: Re: Subject

(87)

I don't get it. How does this make Miranda super-femme? Oh, maybe I do. I know an Indian super-princess, but I forget where she's from. Very femme, but very controlling. Simultaneously wild and straight. It took me a while to get to like her—now I do. (My friend. I don't know if we're quite close enough for friendship.) So you're going with (I don't know if "going with" is the right term for you 'cause then there's Sabina) a princess? Shit, boy. You do step into the meshes. Anyhow, what I'm sure I don't get is how all that she just told me about matriarchy, etc. applies to M's character. I mean, I have the details on one side, not on the other.

Date: Tue, 15 Aug 1995 17:12:20 -0700
From: Acker@eworld.com
To: mwark@laurel.ocs.mq.edu.au
Subject: Re: neo-cons

Oh, it's like the left here. If you can call it "them" that. Cockburn's on the mark on this one. I think he slips in and out of being on the mark and then drunkenness. It's all splintered, here. There's the old new left—as you describe—quite accurately—less and less. Then, the "conservative" left. Again, as you describe. In _The Nation_ this week, a kind of cool article about starting a third party, rather sensible position until it comes to "making alcohol illegal." Oh, America. Make me illegal. Hard enough here to do anything but overwork. Speaking of which, the Blanchot thing-ie is coming up. (I'm getting addicted to bad puns—just did another male-male scene. How to get off in days of depriva-tion.) Oh, back to reality. The left. Then, there are all sorts of rad groups and nutcases, all shifting and shading into each other and into forms of William Buckley, and then there's me and my friends. Confused. Kind of anarchic and too fond of fun. Let's forget "us." There is a kind of base "populism" here…and emerging…every other kind it seems, all mixed up with hatred of intellectuality and other forms of Puritanism. Well, I'm no good at describing this 'cause I'm bad at describing anything not through emotion. So there's a kind of bad try at description.

Date: Tue, 15 Aug 1995 17:13:11 -0700
From: Acker@eworld.com
To: mwark@laurel.ocs.mq.edu.au
Subject: Re: queer as fuck / fuck as queer

Oh…fuck (but you'll never remember what this is a reply to. What a useless reply…)

Date: Tue, 15 Aug 1995 17:38:36 -0700
From: Acker@eworld.com
To: mwark@laurel.ocs.mq.edu.au
Subject: Re: love's executioner

mwark wrote: "Yes, 'equality' in the sense of the double, the exact equal, is a myth. So the ethical question is: how can difference remain fluid, open? Or: which top/bottom relations are *justified*? (The word hierarchy comes from hieros—the sacred, which is what justifies what is justifed)."

− − − End Original Text − − −

This is to remind myself of your last letter. So I don't get confused. What you call difference, I call radical difference. Recognition of. OK so here goes Blanchot. Shit. I'm in a bad mood. In 1935 Breton and Bataille, even now a strange two-some, form Contre-Attaque in response to the actions of fascist militia organizations. Breton stays with Russia, so to speak; the two quarrel. Begin here:

One of Bataille's main concerns was community. According to Blanchot, a close friend, and I think correctly according to Blanchot. Everyone takes Bataille's work to be about ecstasy—I agree with Blanchot that that's wrong.

OK: the second beginning.

1. Bataille, and through Bataille, Blanchot are arguing against totalitarianism, whose forms appear in both fascism and in democracy. (Thus, they, and you and I, are in an untenable position. And here the argument begins. Where can we begin to look for ground, ground for possible community? I think this is ALWAYS Bataille's main question. And so, in his fiction, he throws the

Oedipal model on its head, cuts off the head so to speak, in text or actually, and asserts a totally fascinating OTHER sexual model as ground. By sexual I am also including gender politics. No one, as yet, by the way, as far as I know, and I know several Bataille scholars, has gone over this ground. I fucking love teaching _Story of the Eye_ and after). Oh shit, I always interrupt myself. So, Blanchot: "What about this possibility which, one way or another, is always caught in its own impossibility?" What possibility? That of political/personal community, communitas. "Communism, by saying that equality is its foundation and that there can be no community until the needs of all men are EQUALLY fulfilled (this in itself a minimal requirement), presupposes not a perfect society but a principle of a transparent humanity essentially produced by itself alone, an "immanent" humanity (says Jean-Luc Nancy). The immanence of man to man (sic) also points to man as the absolutely immanent being because he is or has to become such that he might entirely be a work, his work, and, in the end, the work of EVERYTHING...Here lies the seemingly healthy origin of the sickest totalitarianism." Why? Of course, 'cause there's no recognition of radical difference.

So Bataille, and through Bataille, Blanchot turns to the self-other (relation?!) as the possible ground for community. Remember, we are talking about the ground of radical difference. Let's see if I can find one of the essential (essential!?) passages: "A being does not want to be recognized, it (notice the "it") wants to be contested: in order to exist, it goes toward the other, which contests and at times negates it." (He will get more radical than this—all hovering on a discussion of language or of meaning, that loss.) Sorry I'm interrupting again so

I'll repeat, "which contests and at times negates it, so as to start being only in that privation that makes it conscious (here lies the origin of its consciousness) of the impossibility of being itself, as subsisting as its IPSE or, if you will, as itself as a separate individual: this way it will perhaps ex-ist, experiencing itself as an always prior exteriority (look where Foucault takes this up), or as an existence shattered through and through, composing itself only as it decomposes itself constantly, violently, and in silence." Well, there's an even better passage about language: that the more I, as "I," mean or want to say to you, take the example of a lover who wants to tell his lover that he loves him/her, the less you'll understand, and as meaning falls away, as in Blanchot's magnificent fiction, there lies the origin of my consciousness, i.e. I think, "Oh, that's who I am." Radical difference, eh? Well, enough of this: you're probably bored out of your mind. My poor students have to deal with my blatherings, which become worse…Just heard that there's no Dartmouth job…the position didn't come through (not for me specifically, rather not at all). Well, I'm on the road again. Heard from some friends in England in the last few days and said to the last one, June's my deadline. I'm out of here whatever happens. Life's too short not to be lived as fully as possible. Wonder what'll happen next?

Date: Tue, 15 Aug 1995 20:44:31 -0700
From: Acker@eworld.com
To: mwark@laurel.ocs.mq.edu.au
Subject: Re: neo-cons

How about porn? No, I'll be serious and reply later…I'm rushing to a dinner…without my bikes for the night…feels like my cock's been cut off

---

Date: Wed, 16 Aug 1995 10:12:00 +1000 (EST)
From: McKenzie Wark <mwark@laurel.ocs.mq.edu.au>
To: Acker@eworld.com
Subject: Re: Subject

Oh, in Miranda's case it's about *disinheritance* from what is rightfully hers: property, power, respect.

Her father left her and her mother under family pressure. So M has this sense of lost inheritance, in the cultural sense and in the sense of a power that she should have and doesn't. The 'myth of the matriarchy' thing that herbal feminism invents for itself in the west—for her it's real. As for the superfemme traits. I asked her once where she learned how to manipulate men and her answer was: "from four stepfathers."

Sabina, on the other hand, is a butch bottom in spirit but who gets about in superfemme drag. Little black dresses and lipstick. But things are not what they seem!

kx

Date: Wed, 16 Aug 1995 10:19:29 +1000 (EST)
From: McKenzie Wark <mwark@laurel.ocs.mq.edu.au>
To: Acker@eworld.com
Subject: Re: Subject

I've just realised I've lost the plane ticket(!) I get in to SF at 1:40 PM Thurs Sept 14 and leave on 16th at 9:35 am. Yes I'd love to stay with you and I'd love to meet anyone you think I might like/might like me. If you're busy I can look after myself but if you have time I'd like to spend time with you. I will arrange to see Greil Marcus while I'm in town—I don't know if he's yr cup of tea (or mine, for that matter!) but there's only one way to find out. Maybe a late lunch on the 15th or something. I'll fax him and see what's up, but either I can do that or we can both see him, I don't mind. I'll find out when he's free.

kxx

Date: Wed, 16 Aug 1995 10:30:10 +1000 (EST)
From: McKenzie Wark <mwark@laurel.ocs.mq.edu.au>
To: Acker@eworld.com
Subject: Re: neo-cons

I have to write 4,000 words on 'my position' on all this for _Arena Journal_. Yikes! What can one say? How can one say it? I wrote it all in the 2nd person and it comes off too pretentious. So that won't work.

(94)

Also a nightmare is taking a 'position' at QueerLit in a couple of weeks. How to be for the writing that gets writ under the auspices of gay writing but not in favour of Gay Writing…

My only resort is irony, but that's kinda played itself…

kxx

Date: Wed, 16 Aug 1995 10:31:05 +1000 (EST)
From: McKenzie Wark <mwark@laurel.ocs.mq.edu.au>
To: Acker@eworld.com
Subject: Re: queer as fuck / fuck as queer

Oh…fuck.

Seems to me to be a pretty apt reply to just about anything I say…!

kx

Date: Wed, 16 Aug 1995 10:46:52 +1000 (EST)
From: McKenzie Wark <mwark@laurel.ocs.mq.edu.au>
To: Acker@eworld.com
Subject: Re: love's executioner

Certainly not bored with the Blanchot exposition. Fascinated! What were you quoting from? Gotta go teach right now, so I'll think about it later.

Sorry to hear about the Dartmouth job's virtuality not becoming actuality…

kxx

Date: Wed, 16 Aug 1995 17:07:16 +1000 (EST)
From: McKenzie Wark <mwark@laurel.ocs.mq.edu.au>
To: Acker@eworld.com
Subject: Re: neo-cons

How about porn—you mean, as an issue? A lot of the young feminist energy, organised by the Trots, goes into attacking 'representations of women' in mainstream press, billboards. The femocracy is also edging towards tighter community standards in film & literary classification. [Bret Easton Ellis'] _ American Psycho_ had to be sold in clingwrap!

But the really big issue is sexual harassment in the workplace, and (male) university teachers bonking students. *Huge* public debate about a book that deals with a sexual harassment case at Melbourne University. It's put feminism on the front page about 4–5 times this year, which I think has been a pretty good thing.

kx

Date: Wed, 16 Aug 1995 01:48:45 -0700
From: Acker@eworld.com
To: mwark@laurel.ocs.mq.edu.au
Subject: Re: neo-cons

Oh yeah, I heard about that book. Helen Garner. Was going to get it. Fucked-up. I'm totally stinking drunk. Went out to dinner with RU and Paul (from MONDO, ex-MONDO 2000) and this Australian pun...shit!! typing!!! I'm so drunk...publisher, Robert J. Spencer it says on his card MIDNIGHT PUBLISHING, from Perth, some mag like JG, what the fuck, he drank well, all about starting a new mag here, budgets etc., and everyone got dead drunk, like me, and now the boys are doing serious finances so I scooted out. Have to pick up my bike tomorrow so I can head down to LA for five days. Back Monday night (I think) before the work shit hits the fan and I go into major work mode. Vacation over. But not drunkenness. Shit. As for porn. Not issues. What I meant, though it's hard to say what I meant 'cause I'm not quite sober, is that irony's over. Only way to approach an issue is straight-on, of course there's no straight-on says this girl who's lived in London and knows her codes; nevertheless, the way I'd go re all this shit, and it is shit, about straight/gay is straight-on, me it's just straight on romance. That's what I mean by porn. Never writing about something. The distance in the word "about" is always irony. Well, I'm not making sense, as if I know whether I am or not, I shall when sober. I shall. Speaking of straight on, look I think it's really cool that you tell me about your girlfriends. But, as regards, our...whatever... our knowing each other...I think I should be a bit straight. Straight? I'm not exactly sober, but I'll try. I really don't dig

(97)

het (heterosexual) shit when it comes to me. I like hearing about it, but it's another world to me and one which I don't understand. I know this 'cause when I did it, all I did was get hurt. Life's too cool to keep getting hurt and I love my work and my friends and what we do in culture so I don't have time or willingness to go through useless pain anymore. So. Regarding het shit. These games. To me, top/bottom is just stuff that happens in bed. Who fistfucks whom. Outside the bed, I do my work and you do yours. I fucking hate power games outside the bed and have no interest in playing them. I'm being too blunt, but I'm drunk. How does this relate to you and me? From my point of view, we slept together once. Then, it seemed like you no longer wanted to know me. Somehow the sex freaked you out. So I phoned you to tell you that I wanted to get to know you. 'Cause you're of value to me. You're a good person. So we did and are. Getting to know each other. But it's always in my head that you don't know whether or not you want to have sex with me and you have lots of lovers. That makes a power relation between the two of us. 'Cause I'm not ambiguous about you and I'm not sleeping with anyone else at the moment (discounting the play sex I had in Sydney and I never know if RU and I are going to slip and do it again.) So when I say to you you [sic] can either sleep with me or have your own bed in my apartment, etc,. I mean that. I mean, I want to be with you and so you set the terms 'cause that's how the relation so far has been arranged. I'm not fucking playing games. I'm just being straight-forward and trying to be, like good-mannered. Of course, I want to hang with you. My apartment isn't a hotel. I'm trying to be gracious, fuck you. Now if you want me to make the decisions, you have to say so. You see, I'm really not into these out-of-bed games.

Fucking just tell me what you want and I'll go with it. That's what you do when you do s/m scenes. You discuss rules beforehand. 'Cause otherwise it's all too dangerous and there has to be trust. Well, it's the same, for me, with vanilla sex or without sex. If you don't discuss the rules, then the shit power games are outside the bed and they hurt. And I'm truly no longer interested in either hurting or being hurt. It's all boring and I want to work in this world and to matter. I no longer want my time occupied by hurting and being hurt. Sorry for the rave, but sooner or later, I guess something like this needed to be said. Perhaps not so drunkenly. As I said, I think it's totally cool about your girlfriends and what you all do (that's a stupid way to say it, nobody gives anyone else freedom, but…maybe you can sense what I want to mean), but it's not my world. I hear about it, but don't partake. I do like the feeling that we can tell each other things. "Feeling" isn't the right word. But when I say "top" and "bottom" I'm just talking about sexual play. Otherwise, there's just…difference. Real difference. Not fucking games. That's what makes friendship. Oh, I was before quoting from the _Unavowable Commmunity_, Maurice Blanchot (Station Hill Press). If my memory holds. By the way, I slightly know Greil: he adores the Mekons and we met at a gig and then we were on the same panel with Arthur Kroker, my buddy. He and Arthur did not get along. Two roosters. I had my territory so it was easy for me.

Am going to LA Thursday, back Monday night late; on the 28th, off to Chicago for two days to finish up the record.

Date: Wed, 16 Aug 1995 01:53:02 -0700
From: Acker@eworld.com
To: mwark@laurel.ocs.mq.edu.au
Subject: Re: neo-cons

Oh, all that PC feminist shit. man. That used to go on here. What a
bore. Wait 'til girls take over the porn industry. They won't, too many
old sleazy men, but they'll make great inroads. Women discovering
their bodies. Shit. It'll turn things upside- down. You wait. It'll be all
endless ways to orgasm and all this interiorization of victimization will
be over. Ulrike Meinhof was right on that account. It's not women
that men fear, it's the...how do I say this...cessation of the
mind/body split/women. Something like women's bodies. Only if I
say that, I'm back to dualism. Something like menstruation. Reminds
everyone that THE KING MUST DIE (and has). Enough drunken spiel.

Date: Wed, 16 Aug 1995 22:29:34 +1000 (EST)
From: McKenzie Wark <mwark@laurel.ocs.mq.edu.au>
To: Acker@eworld.com
Subject: the important stuff

If I appear to be playing any games, it's not deliberate, it's unthinking.
So I'm sorry about that. I just wanted to indicate that when I met
you, stuff was happening or had happened. I tell stories about myself
through stories about other people. Mostly the women I know,
because they are more interesting than the men!

(100)

It's very simple really: if I'm in SF, I want to see *you*, I want to sleep with *you*. I want a little more of that intimacy, and the *possibility* of sex. If I was sounding evasive or something, I'm sorry about that. I was writing to you from the office and it really wasn't the place or time to think about what I really wanted to say. My cavalier use of this medium. Anyway, aside from all the words, all the words about whatever, it's you that I care about. I want to know you. I want to find a territory with you. I'm not sure what it is, but I want to find it. I'm trying not to presume this or that, but please don't take that to mean indifference or that this is a game to me. But nor do I want to compromise your autonomy where it is vital to you being and becoming what you want.

I'm a bit stuck for what to say next, so I'll leave it at that. Prompt me and I'll come to the point; but I take yr hint about being indirect, not saying up front what I want. I feel like I'm circling around you, trying to spiral in tighter, but not quite knowing what the co-ordinates are. Vertigo. But I'm trying…

kxx

Date: Wed, 16 Aug 1995 22:54:21 +1000 (EST)
From: McKenzie Wark <mwark@laurel.ocs.mq.edu.au>
To: Acker@eworld.com
Subject: Re: neo-cons

The king *is* dead, and buried in Memphis, Tennessee. The black crow king. All the little princes come to dance on his grave. I think yr pointing me towards where the 2nd part of my Elvis essay should go.

Ulrike is right. Or to put it another way, once the Apollonian loses its contours, its form, then it's the women who have the resources for what comes...Dionysus is in the house! But I think the way that ritual originally went is that the women kill Dionysus, like all those screaming teens who cannibalised Elvis, drove him to a living death— and rightly so. And I can't help wanting to be that element in the Dionysian that *wants* to be the sacrifice, so that symbolically at least, MAN IS DEAD. Either his moment in history is finished, or history is finished. Nietzsche's 'hardness'— smashing itself to bits.

The hammer drops, not to the anvil but into the water, where it rusts and rots, yes that's better!

Porn desacralises sex, and that is good. But should something else be made sacred? Does the sacred answer to a need? What if the assigning of sacredness were *arbitrary*? Would that stop it from grounding self-perpetuating powers? I have an intuition that it might be wise to keep something hidden—but what? (What I hate about the Derrideans: they pose as having access to a secret mystery of *language* hidden form those not adept. Deleuze is right: it's a sphinx without a riddle!) But still, Nietzsche poses an interesting question: if God is dead, and of man is dead, what can ground the cultural power of 'our kind'? Thought needs always to go into the world with a few tricks up its sleeve and a dagger in its heart. Or is that the voice of the prince who would be king?

kxx

Date: Wed, 16 Aug 1995 23:16:12 +1000 (EST)
From: McKenzie Wark <mwark@laurel.ocs.mq.edu.au>
To: Acker@eworld.com
Subject: Re: love's executioner

I'm gonna dwell on the Bataille/Blanchot/community thought. (Actually, the problem is that you can't 'dwell' on it). The question that's got me stumped is something like: can community be thought without its encounter with an other? Can it be affirmed? If it can't, then perhaps it's not only an illusion but a needless or dangerous one. Is 'community' where what Nietzsche called the 'shadow of God' is buried? It's a problem for me because obviously I'm supposed to take sides with the culture 'n community people, but I can't *believe*.

Unavowable Community—now there's a concept in a title!

Irony doubled on itself, lost in itself, imploding in on itself—Baudrillard. A burning star pointing to where Bethlehem isn't.

What can come after irony if not deliberate stupidity? To knowingly not self- refer…

kxx

Date: Wed, 16 Aug 1995 12:02:43 -0700
From: Acker@eworld.com
To: mwark@laurel.ocs.mq.edu.au
Subject: Re: neo-cons

This is easier to reply to than the first email so I will. Wait I copied a bit so I wouldn't forget all you wrote. And I have to remember the ending...the prince who would be king..."kill Dionysus, like all those screaming teens who cannibalised Elvis, drove him to a living death—and rightly so. And I can't help wanting to be that element in the Dionysian that *wants* to be the sacrifice, so that symbolically at least, MAN IS DEAD. Either his moment..."

OK. That's to jog my memory. Actually, I can't quite reply, 'cause you've started me pondering and pondering takes time. I totally agree MAN IS DEAD. Though I don't agree about Dionysius. Back to that in a second. But...but but but...this is why I wanted to send you the first two chapters of the new novel...'cause it's on this... what do you (does one) mean by MAN? So we turn to Judith Butler, etc. If, at this point, you do gender essentialism, you, you in particular, a man, find yourself in a mess? You want to be sacrificed? Listen, I'll make position clear both theoretically and outside theory, I am no henchman. So we come to Dionysius. No, the Maenads didn't tear Dionysius apart; rather in the name of Dionysius, and that phrase has to be unraveled, they tore apart the King. And Oedipus. Graves gives an interesting reading of that one. So...are "man" and "woman," for no term in a dual system exists without its complement, in other words, we're in this together, male and female, which is why I shall and will

(104)

not be your henchman. Are "man" and "woman" categories or appearances or phenomena, whatever the correct philosophic term, based on something like Plato's myth of birth (discussion of matter and form)? If so, who are we outside this myth? (Here I take Irigaray and Butler seriously. What I wonder about is Butler's immersion into parody. But that's another topic.) That is, to come down to earth, I have a feeling that we don't know what gender is outside our society...How the fuck could we? (Unless you go back to some kind of essentialism.) That is, the whole way of thinking has to change. We're not going about thinking correctly. So we're finding ourselves in this mess—like wanting to die. To be fucked over. Not loving the joy and power of being alive. It all shits and has to go. There, I've come down to earth. Perhaps the point is that Dionysius was/is not being torn apart and what would it be if "he" was, if the categories inside/outside started spiraling around each other? (As they do during sex).

Re porn. Oh I guess porn as that which is written...oh I'm getting tired of being theoretical. More later. I think I need breakfast.

Date: Wed, 16 Aug 1995 12:07:10 -0700
From: Acker@eworld.com
To: mwark@laurel.ocs.mq.edu.au
Subject: Re: love's executioner

Oh God, you have to read Blanchot. Start with _The Unavowable Community_. That's precisely what the Bataille essay is about. I was hit over the head with it because I felt we now have the same problem "they" did: the simultaneous impossibility of and necessity for community. Community as communion: that's what Bataille and Blanchot can't stand and so they're trying to find the ground for another way of going about, of even "thinking" community. Thus, Bataille descended, so to speak, into the Acephale (that secret community), into the work of Marcel Maus, and so the Collège de Sociologie arose. Well, more on this after breakfast. And must answer your first email and deal with all my confusion.

Date: Wed, 16 Aug 1995 12:09:28 -0700
From: Acker@eworld.com
To: mwark@laurel.ocs.mq.edu.au
Subject: Re: love's executioner

Oh, of course one more thing. "Irony doubling on itself "…well, doesn't language change/have to change as thinking/perceiving does? If God is dead…then we think differently. No longer essentialists. But it's not irony…that way of hopping slipping and sliding…or need not be irony. Blanchot is anything but ironic. Think, the total romance of Marguerite Duras came out of these guys' work. (In the end, I keep finding myself there…lost in romance).

Date: Wed, 16 Aug 1995 12:23:11 -0700
From: Acker@eworld.com
To: mwark@laurel.ocs.mq.edu.au
Subject: Re: the important stuff

Yes, you've had me totally confused. And I still am...'cause emotions take longer to move in me than thought...and I didn't sleep last night. Ever since you didn't come to my reading, I've thought that you weren't terribly interested, at first in getting to know me, then in sleeping with me. That you did sort of find out that you did want to get to know me, perhaps didn't know what to do with it, but decided that you did (want to get to know me). I guess that I do things differently...as I say, I'm a total romantic when let loose. And actually don't sleep around that much—which probably makes things more difficult for me/regarding dealing with me. Better for everyone if I did. But there it is. It's that old s/m thing: one gets too into forms. (Bad childhood and all that, always searching for protection) I wanted/want to get to know you so I decided to let all the sexual ambiguity (is he interested/is he not) slide, a sacrifice I guess to what seemed more important...wanting to...what? ...make something with you. It's hard to not totally misunderstand everything. Like... if you say "I'm coming through SF, and it's basically for 24 hours, I think, well, he doesn't really want to take the time to get to know me, he just wants to get over jetlag and has to do it somewhere...so I plan how to make you most comfortable, get you through jetlag...but confusion (mine) does lead to worse, I guess invariably, to like what just happened, my having to rise up to the surface, through the codes of irony I learned to play in England, and ask

(107)

you directly "What's going on?" Seemed a bit brutal to have to do that so I'm still…perhaps confused…a little in shock. Oh, I can't figure how to get back to your email to read it again. I'll have to go from memory. Well, I do want to sleep with you again and wish we didn't have to hedge around (is that a phrase?) each other so much; I'm not very good with total ambiguity, just want the bit of irony that's always there. I'm very into you.

Date: Wed, 16 Aug 1995 12:27:24 -0700
From: Acker@eworld.com
To: mwark@laurel.ocs.mq.edu.au
Subject: Re: the important stuff

Oh, that's what I wanted to reply to. "The co-ordinates." I don't have a clue. Except I don't want this mess…not knowing anything. That's for sure. Well, I guess the mess is over. As I say. Emotion moves more slowly and more tyrannically than thought (ideas). I guess we'll find the co-ordinates when we come to them. Or, for I don't know your point-of-view, if you have any, co-ordinates are always sort of negative, aren't they? Definers of space, tell me. Oh, I do know that I need to be alone an hour or two every day. But that's not terribly relevant now. As regards my autonomy or career, that's no problem—I'm so tough as regards career that the rock that hits Tantalus wouldn't cause a bruise to this stubborn goat.

Date: Thu, 17 Aug 1995 09:17:59 +1000 (EST)
From: McKenzie Wark <mwark@laurel.ocs.mq.edu.au>
To: Acker@eworld.com
Subject: Re: the important stuff

I'm very into you too. I made all the travel plans just before I met you, and can't change them. So it looks like a flying visit to SF to get over jetlag 'cause that's what it originally was, before I met you. I'm a bit wary about how I'd fit into your space, but I wish it was a little longer than a flying visit. I want to see you again.

kxx

Date: Wed, 16 Aug 1995 21:38:02 -0700
From: Acker@eworld.com
To: mwark@laurel.ocs.mq.edu.au
Subject: Re: the important stuff

Don't worry about how you fit into my space. I don't fit in. It's hopeless. I almost wrote "helpless." There're books and computer equipment everywhere. I'm going to make an effort to order all the shit, but there's just nowhere to put anything anymore. I just don't want to move twice and it's silly to move in this town when I don't know that I want to stay here. So don't judge me by the book-computer-paper mass. It's Hawthorne's Rappaccini's Daughter, that garden time. If you can bear all the books, there's no problem.

I'm off to LA in the morning…my last chance at being on the road on a motorcycle for days before I have to teach again. I've got my teaching down to one long day a week, Tuesday, but it's still a psychic drain so I want to make the most of "freedom" while I can. Plus I'm a bit exhausted from the Australia trip and the road always revives me. I'll be at my friend Matias' on Friday and Saturday, leaving Sunday morning so you can reach me there via (his email) scrollo @aol.com It's totally cool if you do; Matias is almost like a brother to me and very private about my life. On Sunday and Monday I'll just be going from hot spring to hot spring, back here late Tuesday afternoon (before the light gives out). I'm really glad we talked. I was freaking. (oh, I told you about Matias; he works with Dick Hebdige; actually he studied with Derrida, but keeps this quiet. He's really fun to be with and his boyfriend's a cutie.) I'm glad you're coming here.

Date: Wed, 16 Aug 1995 21:44:43 -0700
From: Acker@eworld.com
To: mwark@laurel.ocs.mq.edu.au
Subject: Re: neo-cons

I agree with you, of course. Isn't it funny how we keep returning to Nietzsche? And in a funny way, that lovely myth, "permanent revolution?" But I want to write more when I look at the other letters. By the way, I never thought about drag that way. Makes it much more understandable to me. There are so many drag queens in this town…and some of them just look at you, well, some have at me as if they're judging me, am I good enough to be "a real woman"? So there's some tension. 'Cause they do the stuff I don't want to do: all the high heels and make-up and wiggle…it was all so oppressive to me. A real lesson in otherness—yes? It's cool what you say about drag. I always find "women's stuff" hard 'cause it makes me feet too vulnerable: dressing like a guy and living among gym geeks and motorcycles makes me feel safe. Yet I don't feel butch when I do this. Isn't all this stuff weird: the way everything (sign) is always reversing itself?

Date: Wed, 16 Aug 1995 21:49:32 -0700
From: Acker@eworld.com
To: mwark@laurel.ocs.mq.edu.au
Subject: Re: neo-cons

Why's Elvis "the black crow king"? But I'm not a big Elvis freak so I don't know. I like Sphinxes without riddles 'cause I like those moments when the mind almost…(I feel like I'm reverting to Bataille)…disappears…a Sphinx without riddles makes it happen. I don't know why we separate the "sacred" from "everyday." When I was in Haiti, it was all the same…I felt as if my brain, to exist there, had to reverse itself, rather, invert, and start working that way…I had to "think" totally differently. I would ask directions, for instance, and whoever I asked would answer, "This path is bad" or "This path is good." The word "because" meant nothing. I liked it there. (Though, politically, it was a total horror show.)

(111)

Date: Wed, 16 Aug 1995 21:52:22 -0700
From: Acker@eworld.com
To: mwark@laurel.ocs.mq.edu.au
Subject: Re: love's executioner

Ah, deliberate stupidity. That's what I missed. Someone told me that _The Simpsons_translates to outside USA, but _Beavis and Butthead_ doesn't. All very peculiar and interesting. Somehow, for me, _Beavis and Butthead_ hits it on the head. An unfortunate turn-of-phrase. Stupidity, so clear that it no longer be totally conscious, is/was definitely one movement after punk. I understand that.

Date: Wed, 16 Aug 1995 22:00:57 -0700
From: Acker@eworld.com
To: mwark@laurel.ocs.mq.edu.au
Subject: Re: the important stuff

This is almost like chatting. I certainly don't expect to hear from you re Matias; it's just my habit of saying where I am 'cause I tour so much if I don't do that I'm sort of nowhere. I'll have to introduce you to motorcycles...one of the last myths left. Actually I think they're coming back. Perhaps what you're referring to as the sacred.

Cool re your comfort with books. I have thousands.

Date: Wed, 16 Aug 1995 22:03:48 -0700
From: Acker@eworld.com
To: mwark@laurel.ocs.mq.edu.au
Subject: Re: neo-cons

I prefer disavowal of being man. Or of man. 'Cause drag as per-
fection of the feminine makes me hate the feminine even
more…I don't want that. But then… sometimes…I fetishize the
masculine…spreading legs and drinking beer and grunting…and
sweating and being stupid and rubbing your crotch…it turns me
on. Must be sort of a mirror…(Am I being clear?) I've got to get
over my fears around the feminine…oh all this shitty past…the
sexist society past.

Date: Wed, 16 Aug 1995 22:52:51 -0700
From: Acker@eworld.com
To: mwark@laurel.ocs.mq.edu.au
Subject: Re: neo-cons

Explain. Why Elvis' death and our problem with the sacred? A huge
problem, I think, not only looking at my own life but at what's happening here, (in the USA), has been for a while…that hole or black
mass (what an awful pun) that has led to all the right-wing Christian
stuff, among other things…

Date: Wed, 16 Aug 1995 22:58:58 -0700
From: Acker@eworld.com
To: mwark@laurel.ocs.mq.edu.au
Subject: Re: love's executioner

Isn't that interesting about lyricism? To me, having had a huge problem writing the Mekons' songs, yes, that's what it is, and I kept thinking, I can't do this, it's (like) having to get something that just isn't there, and then…sometimes…it just happens, i.e. the 'thing' is there…too much like inspiration to suit me. Too sharp. Fiction writing I like better 'cause you just write and write, work, I know work, and then shape it down, rework it, and extract the hot stuff. If you do enough, there's hot stuff. But lyricism…you have to come on it. Light on it. Very hard. Me, I like stupid. I think that's one of the bases for my relation with RU. I think it's an American 'thang'…oh I'm edging on an essentialism, a cultural one, oh yuck…but (fact or phenomenon) it makes me laugh. For instance, when I was living in London, what I missed most about "Here" was wrestling. I fucking love American wrestling when I'm out of the States. The best performance art.

Date: Thu, 17 Aug 1995 10:28:27 +1000 (EST)
From: McKenzie Wark <mwark@laurel.ocs.mq.edu.au>
To: Acker@eworld.com
Subject: Re: neo-cons

When Foucault talks about 'man' making his exit, I think he is showing it to be a shadow of the category 'God.' After the death of God we live with God's shadows, but they too are disappearing from the earth. Only some of those shadows are more durable than others, like nation, community, culture, and the great American self.

So it's not that male bodies have to die, but to some extent male bodies are a good basis for the ritual sacrifice of Man. It's one of the things drag sometimes aspires to. It's a refusal that draws attention to what it refuses.

To some extent, it's only if men have the will to overcome Man that anything much can be achieved. Which, incidentally, is why I think separatism has its limitations. It affirms the other, not itself. Separatism is a sacrifice to the greater glory of Man. The refusal of the categories is in the long run more important than the affirmation of the opposite pole, be it a feminist or a gay separatism.

kxx

Date: Thu, 17 Aug 1995 14:50:27 +1000 (EST)
From: McKenzie Wark <mwark@laurel.ocs.mq.edu.au>
To: Acker@eworld.com
Subject: Re: the important stuff

Have a great trip! I can't imagine being *revived* by long distance motorcycling, but...

(115)

It sounds like your apartment is something like my apartment, so I'll fit in to the space just fine! Books? Did somebody say book?! I'm going to hunt down that Blanchot and have a read of it while you're away.

I think we're sort of getting somewhere in the dialogue and that's good. If I don't write to you c/o yr friend don't worry, I'll be here when you get back!

kxx

Date: Thu, 17 Aug 1995 14:53:12 +1000 (EST)
From: McKenzie Wark <mwark@laurel.ocs.mq.edu.au>
To: Acker@eworld.com
Subject: Re: neo-cons

I like drag as The Man's idea of the feminine—perfected. But I like it even more as a disavowal of being Man. I'm interested in this 'cause of the Warhol thing I'm planning.

kxx

Date: Thu, 17 Aug 1995 14:56:17 +1000 (EST)
From: McKenzie Wark <mwark@laurel.ocs.mq.edu.au>
To: Acker@eworld.com
Subject: Re: neo-cons

There's a Nick Cave song called 'the Black Crow King,' which is on the same record as his John Lee Hooker meets Elvis thing.

Actually I'm completely indifferent to Elvis musically. I chose to write about him on Duchampian grounds—indifference. But I've come to think of his death as a touchstone for the modern problem of the sacred.

kxx

Date: Thu, 17 Aug 1995 14:59:31 +1000 (EST)
From: McKenzie Wark <mwark@laurel.ocs.mq.edu.au>
To: Acker@eworld.com
Subject: Re: love's executioner

The _Simpsons_ is still ironic. _Beavis and Butthead_ is just, well, stupid! It would play here if we had MTV, but we don't. Simpsons is broadcast culture, B&B is cable. In the broadcast world, cable is viewed with intense fear and loathing.

I'm not really equipped as a writer to do stupid. But I can do lyricism—the flattening out of the surface of the prose to a *simple* emotion. Hide all the rest in the architecture.

Date: Thu, 17 Aug 1995 16:22:57 +1000 (EST)
From: McKenzie Wark <mwark@laurel.ocs.mq.edu.au>
To: Acker@eworld.com
Subject: Re: neo-cons

Well, you do a better job of the man thing than I do, I think. I'm always intensely uncomfortable with the physical side of masculinity. But I think I overcompensate by throwing my weight around on the page and when speaking in public. (About the only person with whom I've not said my piece lately is the prime minister, oh, and Sandy Stone, who for interesting reasons seems to create a bit of a no-go zone around herself.)

kxx

Date: Thu, 17 Aug 1995 16:27:29 +1000 (EST)
From: McKenzie Wark <mwark@laurel.ocs.mq.edu.au>
To: Acker@eworld.com
Subject: Re: neo-cons

In what I've already written on Elvis, he's the sacrifice to the recording of breath, the theft of breath by the dead world of recording. But I'm starting to think now about Elvis also as the sacrifice that marks the end of community, as the anti- Christ in terms of time. The crucifixion is supposed to inaugurate community, but it think Elvis is a kind of profane double.

You know the way fish breed: squirting eggs and sperm into the water. Culture is the water of the machines, the medium in which they breed...(this is my Marxist soul speaking: the pathos of the overcoming of the living by the products of their labours, by dead labour...)
kxx

Date: Thu, 17 Aug 1995 16:30:38 +1000 (EST)
From: McKenzie Wark <mwark@laurel.ocs.mq.edu.au>
To: Acker@eworld.com
Subject: Re: love's executioner

There definitely is a certain kind of stupidity that American culture has raised to a fine art. It's not an essence, but it is a phenomena. Baudrillard again: leave irony to the Europeans; American art is best when it's like the desert or like crystal.

kxx

Date: Thu, 17 Aug 1995 10:57:13 -0700
From: Acker@eworld.com
To: mwark@laurel.ocs.mq.edu.au
Subject: Re: neo-cons

Fuck, I woke up late due to no sleep the night before…not much time to get to where I'm going today and all this email (business stuff). Oh, I'll eat a big breakfast. What the hell. And ride through the night. I'm a sleep junky. No time to rereply now but I want to ask you more questions about Elvis. I'll just keep this letter in open till I return. Re pissing people off in public: I've noticed that I have this perverse streak, I have many but this one I hate. Oh shit there's the tea. What a foul mouth I have—Lord knows where my favorite words fuck and shit every entered during my so-called ritzy upbringing. Perverse streak: re every now and then becoming a brat, in public, when, if I kept myself down, I'd get the gig, or whatever's a stake. I'm not capable of saying anything today: I'm off !!! Trees and sun right in my face and wind and boring roads and cool, slow turning roads, then, a quick turn, like doing an amazing ballet. Oh. Flying. Oh, one thing. Listen, please, don't understand my freaking out yesterday as having anything to do with you talking about your friends and lovers. I love that; then, I can talk too. What bothers me, i.e. has the potential to bother me, bother isn't the right word, is when things aren't right between us. I'm not saying this properly, I'm using clichés, oh well. What's between us is just that and has nothing to do with your relations with other people. We both live in the world and I like that. This is all said horribly and with no attention to problems of identity, self and other. Using old definitions. I can't help it—I'm off! Out of this town! yay! I'm glad we talked...In five days...Elvis...(but I want something else than sacrifice...or than... Christian sacrifice...)

Date: Thu, 17 Aug 1995 11:32:32 -0700
From: Acker@eworld.com
To: mwark@laurel.ocs.mq.edu.au
Subject: Re: love's executioner

Can't help asking this before I go. Over not big but great breakfast, reading a hilarious article on Gingrich in the new _New York Review of Books_. (I rant against this and _The Nation_ but I read them religiously. Perverse.) Article of Gingrich's stupidity. Basically. Question: why is this guy able to take, one wouldn't even say views, for they're less or lower than that, and turn them into major policy in the USA? (Not that "he's" the one who "doing" or "making" the change.) Why this stupidity now? That's the question. It's not the old-boy regime of Bush or the Mafia- hook-up of Nixon: this is something else. I don't understand.

Date: Fri, 18 Aug 1995 13:25:52 +1000 (EST)
From: McKenzie Wark <mwark@laurel.ocs.mq.edu.au>
To: Acker@eworld.com
Subject: Re: neo-cons

(121)

I think the problem was me talking about various emotional ties I have with certain people in the *absence* of talking about my emotional ties to you. I was deferring something until I found the words...but one never finds the words.

I'm reading Blanchot's _Le Pas Au-Delà_, which I can barely understand at all. Altho' I can relate to it through the Deleuzian take on the eternal return as the return of difference. Blanchot has clearly read Deleuze on this and does something else with it.

Had breakfast with Paul Patton, who translated Deleuze's _Difference & Repetition_, and he cleared up a few things for me. My intuition that the Australian 'postmodern republic' idea is something like Blanchot's impossible community seems to have something in it after all.

Hopefully I'll have some clearer thoughts by the time you get back. kxx

---

Date: Sat, 19 Aug 1995 03:27:51 -0400
From: Kathyacker@aol.com
To: mwark@laurel.ocs.mq.edu.au
Subject: hello from LA

You've got to read _Theorem_ (Pasolini)—more and more fascinating—Verso, especially the poem in the middle—so I can talk to you about it. All this stuff on Adam, Eve, and sacrifice. I'm not sure that I'm getting it.

A.

Date: Sun, 20 Aug 1995 00:15:07 +1000 (EST)
From: McKenzie Wark <mwark@laurel.ocs.mq.edu.au>
To: Kathyacker@aol.com
Subject: Re: hello from LA

Teorama—I have it on video and might have the book still. I think I gave it to someone. But I'll locate it, anyway.

It's been so strange, not writing to you for, what? 72 hours?

kxx

Date: Sun, 20 Aug 1995 15:59:10 -0400
From: Kathyacker@aol.com
To: mwark@laurel.ocs.mq.edu.au
Subject: Re: hello from LA

I'm weirding out from not emailing with you—having a wonderful time, as the postcards say, but weirding out. Two more days till I return to email. Sigh. I have to see the movie again—there's this poem in the middle of the book about Adam and Eve, really about the female's, or girl's, position in the world from Pasolini's(?) point-of-view. Or it's another discussion of loss (the book keeps shifting themes and yet remains crystal clear—a Blanchot foil). I want to ask you about it. I miss you.

Date: Mon, 21 Aug 1995 07:40:54 +1000 (EST)
From: McKenzie Wark <mwark@laurel.ocs.mq.edu.au>
To: Kathyacker@aol.com
Subject: Re: hello from LA

I miss you too. But I haven't got that far in the book yet.

kxx

Date: Tue, 22 Aug 1995 17:42:10 -0700
From: Acker@eworld.com
To: mwark@laurel.ocs.mq.edu.au
Subject: Re: neo-cons

I'm back. Beautiful ride today…and then hit fog just as I approached SF. Cold and wet. Typical. (I typed 'topical' by mistake. I love typos.) I'm sure you don't remember your message of the 17th. And here I am

(124)

replying. (You said two things: one, re Blanchot, something in the stuff around community, your discussion of community and his. Boy, am I not being clear. I can't repeat your words.) Anyhow, yes, I think there's something. I wanted to reread Blanchot this vacation, read some new essays, but got simultaneously bogged down and fascinated by the Pasolini with Matias. Oh dear. We'll have to pick a Blanchot text together...(for my sake)...but meanwhile there's Pasolini.

My parentheses have gone to hell. What happens after 300 miles on a bike. The second thing you said: regarding your always discussing your emotions about your girlfriends, but not about me—that being a problem. You see—I'm awful at paraphrasing you. Your words. Well, sweetie, I'm probably worse than you. And telephones—I can't handle those things at all. I wish we could spend some days together. Perhaps in the future. Time is so weird...emailing now, I feel like the time between your email and this is usual email time: time elapsed. Five days never happened. I think I'm a little scared of you 'cause you're a guy; if you were a girl, I'd just blurt things out. Also I don't want to trespass: you have a complicated life and I don't want...I don't know...it's really just fear. Anyhow, yes. Maybe that's a problem too, your talking about your girlfriends all the time, but I also think it's cool 'cause I'm getting to know you that way and I like when knowledge (or misknowledge) is complicated...Oh well, you'd better reply or my tongue will tie itself into even more knots and I'll never be able to eat again.

So I took some 'shrooms last night (Matias was going to come up to the hot springs with me but his car broke down and I didn't want to

(125)

waste the mushroom). It didn't do much; I fell into a sort of sleep, part hallucination?, around twelve and woke up two hours later— wait, I wrote this down…you're lying dead under water. I had to explain who you are to the reporters. What I remember is that it was magical, swimming under all that water, and your 'deadness' was sort of magical too. But I don't have a clue what this was about, if it was dream or hallucination…(the actual message I wrote to myself was: Ken dead under water who is he? find out for reporters) I must have been stoned.

Got this weird fax from Danielle Talbot when I returned (did I tell you about Danielle, a bit of a story, she reports for _The Age_)—all about how Liz Porter of the _Sunday Age_ hates my guts and then some indecipherable copy of an article and then Danielle asking me if I want Sheila Jeffries job—if so, Danielle, I quote, "will start lobbying"—thought you'd be amused.

When you said you were dishing everyone but the Prime Minister and…someone else, to what were you referring? Send copies, yes? I want to read what you write. And what happened re the article that mentioned Sabina? Did you cause trouble…?

(My bleach is dripping down my fax. I'll have to get off.) Shit. This isn't a very academic email. I'll be more interesting next time. I need new books to read. Oh shit, it's getting in my eyes. Why am I so set on having white hair? Oh, I was trying to read _The Work Of Fire_ (Blanchot). But it got boring. And Robbe-Grillet started to amuse. (Going back to my childhood there. Pure obsession. Maybe I'll read

Duras again—the ultimate candy.) Oh, I know. I know what I keep forgetting to mention. All about my friend at the Getty. Roberto [Bedoya] who runs the community affairs at the Getty Institute. And David Jensen who does the more national stuff. I kept telling them about your book. Are copies available in this country? I also want Larry Rickels (who always gets Theweleit to teach at UCSB) to see it too.

Date: Tue, 22 Aug 1995 19:41:36 -0700
From: Acker@eworld.com
To: mwark@laurel.ocs.mq.edu.au
Subject: Re: neo-cons

mwark wrote: "irony, but that something can disrupt that detachment that it will nevertheless be unable to reject: the return of the innocent. The unmediated relation of the body to itself as innocence. Which is also for Pasolini I think the significance of Christ crucified. The body as pure exposure. That the return of the sacred has to do with the body as uninflected presence. But why."

— — — End Original Text — — —

This is just so I can remember. Am supposed to go to this birthday party now but it's at a pizza place and I hate pizza. So I'm being a baby and writing you instead.

The strange thing, well there are a lot of strange things, but the strange thing that's sitting in my mind now is that about three years ago I read this third part to _The Story of O_, in the usual Blue Noon edition. In this one, O has become a sort of dom, enters a bourgeois family, and seduces everyone. Now I realize that this "porn" book isn't a reply of what it says it is _The Story of O_, but rather of _Theorem_(the Pasolini text). Only the "stranger" is a woman. Why is this strange for me? Something to do with innocence. Which is why I copied your text. Something is on the tip of my mind...I don't know what. Something I want to get at. About innocence. I'm sitting here searching for the next step in the writing I'm doing... Dionysus isn't good enough...why?...the story reeks too much of guilt, male angst...why do I say "male"...I think that by "female" I mean something to do with "innocence"...now this is strange...I'm hunting, here, Ken; I don't know or understand precisely what I'm saying 'cause I have to feel before I understand...something, innocence, sounds right. Of course, the body. Laura A's gorgeous body in _The Leopard_, no, the D'Annunzio based film _The Innocent_. There must be voluptuousness. What the hell do I mean by that? At least you always know what you mean. Back to what you were saying...about the father. The son hidden in the father. Reminds me of Plato's cave myth. That women have no part in generation, for they do not/cannot partake of form. Something like that. The body must be what is innocent, for the body is that which changes, dies, corrupts. To see. Something to do with seeing. But about the father? That's hard for me. You'll have to explain men to me.

(128)

Oh the dream was much richer than that. Not death like "X dies"; no, more a Argento film, like the scene in _Inferno_ when the girl searches for the key she has just dropped in a pool and the pool goes into water without depth. Shit, I can't type. (It always looks like I can't spell. I can't bear to read what I've written 'cause I'll have to rewrite…)

Date: Tue, 22 Aug 1995 23:11:38 -0700
From: Acker@eworld.com
To: mwark@laurel.ocs.mq.edu.au
Subject: Re: neo-cons

I think this is all very dubious. Why do you want "immanence"? And of all things, the body. Sure, that's the whole Oedipal myth— read Stephen Pfohl's discussion of doubling in _Paradise Cafe_ (St Martin's). I think Stephen has a point (a point! what a metaphor!). This is precisely what Blanchot is arguing against—he's saying that immanence is as belief a ground for totalitarianism. Why the fuck do men want to be "the king who doesn't die" (the false sign that hides the reality of the king-murder, the basis of society, according to Bataille)? This is what I don't get? And why this appropriation in my, the female name? I.e. this desire to be sure that the body is never object. I love being someone's object. I love being wanted. My body wanted. And wrongly. "Come here, slave." It's one of the sexiest things I know. Totally not equal to "You're a victim." Perhaps the sacred has something to do not with immanence but with disap-pearance. (Even with rejection.) What an awful thing—to want the

(129)

power not to die. To see that as freedom. And, worse, as "my" free-dom, as what I as woman want. No way. I'm very good at saying what I want (though helpless at getting it/her/him). (I don't like this essentialism—me as "woman"—but I'm using it for argument's sake.) So I don't know about this body as body. One can't argue solely from the rational, one has to account for experience, ESPE-CIALLY in the realm of the body. That's where sex so amazes me: what delights me is so often what I never suspected. And it may not again. And…there seem to be few, if any, rules. One day one way, one day another. I never know. That's it—that fabulous not knowing. One may look at another's body, or parts, as objects. It's the rigidity that bothers me: the "always this way." Perhaps what you are saying in regard to immanence is true within the area of patriarchy…but but but.

Date: Wed, 23 Aug 1995 10:52:47 +1000 (EST)
From: McKenzie Wark <mwark@laurel.ocs.mq.edu.au>
To: Acker@eworld.com
Subject: Re: neo-cons

So nice to hear from you! Have to go teach right this second. I'll be back later…

kxx

Date: Wed, 23 Aug 1995 12:16:22 +1000 (EST)
From: McKenzie Wark <mwark@laurel.ocs.mq.edu.au>
To: Acker@eworld.com
Subject: Re: neo-cons

I'm imagining me lying dead in the water and reporters and you know what I come up with: _Sunset Boulevard_! Overrated film, but the talking corpse idea is pure Billy Wilder. Apparently the original opening was in a morgue, all these corpses popping out of their slots in the wall with stories to tell. The studio nixed it as too bizarre.

Theorem is an interesting book. Usual Pasolini blend of Marx, Freud and Mediterranean Christianity. I think of him mostly as a Christian heretic. The church paid very little attention to communist writers at the time, except Pasolini. Precisely because he was speaking as a Christian against the Church. No wonder he published a set of essays called Lutheran letters. I like the idea of the danger of innocence returning, and resulting in art, madness, sainthood among the dependents. That bourgeois consciousness necessarily lives in a certain detachment from itself, in a certain irony, but that something can disrupt that detachment that it will nevertheless be unable to reject: the return of the innocent. The unmediated relation of the body to itself as innocence. Which is also for Pasolini I think the significance of Christ crucified. The body as pure exposure. That the return of the sacred has to do with the body as uninflected presence. But why only male bodies? That poem tries for a justification of this in abstract terms, rather than in terms of Pasolini's personal taste!

(131)

There is something in that notion of the voluptuous presence of the body of the (potential or actual) father. Who can claim to see it as an object, as a possession? In Pasolini's world—nobody. A woman's body too easily becomes an object *for* the viewer, for the father. But the father's body...I think Pasolini wants to reveal this as hidden within the order of the signifier, within the patriarchal symbolic order. Hidden within it is the pure, exposed body of the *absolute son* (who in the gospels is both son of man/son of God).

I suspect that for Pasolini _The Gospel of Matthew_ and _Teorama_ are essentially the same film.

I'm guessing but maybe there's something of a parallel between some of your stuff and Pasolini at the level of a strategy for working within certain discursive spaces, altho' the spaces themselves couldn't be more different. And also that his is a formalism of structure rather than method.

Other stuff, I'll have to come back to. Is my book available in the US? Should be, but it's easier if I have copies sent to people. So if you give me the addresses I'll have copies sent to anyone you think might find it interesting. What else was there? I'll have to come back to other stuff later. But it's nice to be talking to you again. It was strange talking to you on the phone 'cause we've never done it, but it was really good to hear your voice again.

kxx

Date: Wed, 23 Aug 1995 13:20:34 +1000 (EST)
From: McKenzie Wark <mwark@laurel.ocs.mq.edu.au>
To: Acker@eworld.com
Subject: Re: neo-cons

I'm thinking about Jarman as much as Pasolini, and I'm trying to juxtapose *exposure* to *transgression*. This picks up from talking to Michael Hardt at Virtual Futures, who gave a paper on a Pasolini poem about the crucifixion. This notion of exposure is I think interesting because it also takes the crucified male body out of the realm of the transcendent. It's the pure immanence of the body becoming itself, unfolding itself *without reference* to the other. It just is, for itself. Now, if the female body does this, the other appropriates it as object. But if it's a male body, then in a sense it's protected from being an object by the fact that there is this transcendental myth attached to it. So even in revealing the hidden imminent voluptuousness of the body, hiding within the transcendent myth, it uses that myth as the cover, to prevent the body thus slipping into being an object for the other. (Which it often does in Genet, for example.) What's the etymology of the word 'voluptuous'? It seems like a strange word in English. Where does it come from? I'll look it up later. I'm a great believer in etymology...

How can a body become something out of itself, as pure imminence, rather than in relation to the other? That's the question. Stuart Hood hints at the Spinozism in _ Theorem_, but thinks it's simply a matter of style. But it might go further than that... kxx

Pussy, King of the Pirates

Kathy Acker

the rats eat everything

into the dead
morass of bones
and living eyes

xxx boygirl cemetery
xxx in ocean

(me)

dead skunk territory

the rules of ownership

sunken pirate ship

be with me

vicious crabs

waiting for you

GROVE PRESS
New York

we don't use words here

sex

a box

Drawing by Kathy Acker in a copy of the galleys for *Pussy, King of the Pirates* that she gave to Ken Wark in San Francisco.

Date: Mon, 12 Feb 1996 12:57:26 -0800
From: Acker@eworld.com
To: mwark@laurel.ocs.mq.edu.au
Subject: Re: another day in the saltmines

Just read this over breakfast: I too am returning from Zirma: my memory includes dirigibles flying in all directions, at window level; streets of shops where tattoes are drawn on sailors' skin; underground trains crammed with obese women suffering from the humidity. My traveling companions, on the other hand, swear they saw only one dirigible hovering among the city's spires, only one tattoo artist arranging needles and inks and pierced patterns on his bench, only one fat woman fanning herself on a train's platform. Memory is redundant: it repeats signs so that the city can begin to exist.

Every time you dream I am fucking you, this is what happens.

Afterword by John Kinsella

Hi, K

I have abandoned my somewhat academic introduction to the letters volume, and have decided an email (Acker: 'this isn't a very academic email') that can be used as an intro or an afterword (if you wish) will serve better, and be more honest to the presentation or maybe even manifestation of the *e*-pistolary exchange between you and Kathy Acker. Below, you will find many convention-breakers, including a wild use of parenthesis, and the address (to you?) will be unstable (how else can it be…so?) but how does Acker put it? 'My parentheses have gone to hell.'…*remember*, that was from riding her motorbike for hundreds of miles, and mine are because I've been wandering around in the bush under the wheatbelt sun!

Rereading I came across this from Acker: 'I'm sorry, Ken; do be my friend.' I understand this. I am pretty sure I know what she means outside of the platitudinous. That is, she really does want a friend. Not friends, she has them, but a particular friend. Maybe she has many particular friends, but not this particular one. Is this the key to unlock your exchange? Your almost-love letters of cultural slippage and affirmation? A deep desire to connect: aerially, rhizomically, physically, textually.

I know you reasonably well (or did) in some ways, and in other ways, not at all. I recall, when I first met you, saying, 'I'm not much of a blokey bloke,' and you understood. Do you recall? Then later we interviewed each other about space, wastage, masculinity, travel, and non-belonging. I never met Kathy Acker in the flesh, but felt I knew her (as you'll see in what's to come I feel there's a knowing through text: dangerous as that is!), but was really (really) into her work during the '80s. People used to introduce themselves with, Hey, I heard you are into Acker, so am I. Then it faded from view for me, until I re-engaged with it via *Pussy, King of the Pirates* and *In Memoriam to Identity*. And that has faded a little, though my first encounters never truly will: *Blood and Guts* and *Kathy Goes to Haiti*: I wrote a poem about that and wanted to send it to her but had no idea how. (I was young then, very young. Now, ago) and Acker is long dead. After she died, you wrote a piece for me at my request (for a journal I was editing). I quote it here:

> Escape from the functionaries of language—that is how she understood the literature of the avant garde. One day she will be recognised as a marvellous addition to the escape routes it pioneered. Her writing didn't owe much to Woolf or Stein, but like them, she wrote as a woman, inventing what that might be as she went along.
>
> Being Kathy Acker was, I suspect, not an easy thing. Like Burroughs, she discovered that when you set writing

free, you become even more aware of every little subtle fascism at work in the world. Like Burroughs, she was a visionary writer. Her early books describe the nightmare to come. But they also chart the routes out of the nightmare. ('The Sailor Turned into the Sea' by McKenzie Wark)

And I remember her writing about her illness for the *Guardian*, though Tracy remembers it better. Which brings me to memory, which is what this is all about in so many ways. And because the emails pile up on each other in a way that snailmail letter-writing really couldn't, unless servants or confidants were running messages between great houses back and forth, back and forth, sneaking them into palms behind backs, or leaving carelessly in the foyer for others to steam open and read. Yes, memory, because your few days with Kathy (if I may—seems ungainly in a non-constructive and disempowering way to say 'Acker'; especially given that as reader we're offered the intimacy of the 'strange attractor' mode of email) resonate immediately afterwards on so many temporal levels. Time means loss in so many ways. And in recalling memories of intimacy is the almost desperate desire to gain knowledge of the 'other,' to get to know them. You say to her: 'I want to know you' and she replies, 'I'm very into you.' They are not one and the same thing, but parallel lines bend and touch here and there and confound any science. But you also affirm that you're very into her, and that struggle—it is a struggle—is the anxiety below this almost manic exchange. Though Kathy isn't in a relationship at the time of this exchange, you are, and both of you have to configure a language and nomenclature to embody what it is you're 'doing' with each

(139)

other. You will come to say to her: 'I think the problem was me talking about various emotional ties I have with certain people in the absence of talking about my emotional ties to you. I was deferring something until I found the words…but one never finds the words.'

But memory is a lie and you 'find' this, or always knew it. Playing along as it got more and more real, in the getting to know, ceasing to become the mnemonic extension we all play, the calling out the drag-self (okay, it is the best way of de-masking so often), you go through the dramatic curve of a fiction. It's very Henry James. It covers all the categories of Northrop Frye. And your dénouement? Well, I won't give away the final line, but almost there, you will say: 'Memory is redundant: it repeats signs so that the city can begin to exist.' And this exchange is about being or becoming or unbecoming 'boy and girl,' and about emotions replacing other emotions and priorities, and who occupies what space and how that space is defined, and the grand problem of time: duration and Genettean narratology. Kathy will write, 'The second thing you said: regarding you're always discussing your emotions about your girlfriends, but not about me—that being a problem. You see—I'm awful at paraphrasing you. Your words. Well, sweetie, I'm probably worse than you. And telephones—I can't handle those things at all. I wish we could spend some days together. Perhaps in the future. Time is so weird…emailing now, I feel like the time between your email and this is usual email time: time elapsed. Five days never happened.'

There is a critique of the politics of confrontation with one's own definings outside those imposed by a reactionary social order.

To hold oneself to task, to scrutinise the obsession to self-label, self-differentiate, to contest the internal and external man. You both 'struggle' with this. Both take affirmative self-action. Self-discussion comes with its baggage, though, and Kathy fears (and constantly refers to) her narcissism while embracing it. Like an apologia but only because she is not quite certain enough of you yet: one feels she will become so, and that term/'definition' (category error) will become an in-joke. She is no more and no less than we are expected to be (by ourselves, by media, by all mirrors):

> I prefer disavowal of being man. Or of man. Cause drag as perfection of the feminine makes me hate the feminine even more…I don't want that. But then…sometimes…I fetishise the masculine…spreading legs and drinking beer and grunting…and sweating and being stupid and rubbing your crotch…it turns me on. Must be sort of a mirror…(Am I being clear?) I've got to get over my fears around the feminine…oh all this shitty past…the sexist society past.

Yes, 'struggle.' It seems pivotal in this new epistolary confrontation, affirmation and declaration of love and empathy. There's a dialectic of gender and sexuality, of the American and the non-American, the former stating hers is a country of war and the latter declaring the generic love his social coordinates direct towards it in all its manifestly perverse destiny. Each undoes the codes, but at times each misreads the signals. Funny, in some ways maybe I know you better and always will: the lust for irony to contradict oneself, to be the media plaything while unpicking its rhizomes. I've moved away in recent years, gone down the dreaded Derridean path—though I might add that he shadows your exchange with Kathy in so many ways. The 'struggle'—yes, for 'tops and bottoms,' for 'butch and femme,' for the real man and the aggressive über-fem woman who is a 'ball-breaker.' But as Kathy says, she's not interested in such power games outside the bed. She says: 'Regarding het shit. These games. To me, top/bottom is just stuff that happens in bed. Who fistfucks whom. Outside the bed, I do my work and you do yours. I fucking hate power games outside the bed and have no interest in playing them. I'm being too blunt, but I'm drunk.'

Really, power is an indescribable monster you both spent your time unpicking in its pain and damage, and differentiating forms of pain and damage. Acker wrote to you: 'Community as communion: that's what Bataille and Blanchot can't stand and so they're trying to find the ground for another way of going about, of even "thinking" community.'

Both in your struggle with the sacred, the new sacred of Elvis's death and the simulacra of money in Warhol (yes, why so neglected?), the acts of believing and for you, Ken, very specifically unbelieving or de-believing. But it was the sacred re-embodied in the media, transmuted via Nietszche (you and Kathy do always go back to him!). Media was Kathy's angst and plaything; it was her instrument as it was yours, wanting to be the fool rather than the pundit, the accepted critic. To be inside and watch the government's cabinet members grapple with desire and how in fact they could get it to work. Media. I have no social democrat in me; you do. I only have the anarchist, that bit of you that gnaws away. You write, amidst all your necessary and desired contradictions: 'Media is my obsession, see, and it's an ongoing aesthetic experiment. I'm an artist and my chosen materials are the media. So there's a politics and an aesthetics. And a fascination. I'm trying to get beyond Debord and Baudrillard...I'm a leftwing columnist (a fifth columnist!) in a Murdoch paper...'

You wanted America and you're in America now. Of America, looking back to Australia. You say, 'I can't possibly explain the "America question" in Australian culture, only there might be something in the idea of an essay on it that comes at it the other way around—the Australia problem in American culture. I mean, we never get any attention! We love from afar.' Irony of course; but wait, there's more.

Later in this exchange (late, what has passed to this point? a week or just over, since you were first together?!—you will at one stage say 'It's been so strange, not writing to you for, what? 72 hours?'), you are able to say, out of your 'wonderment' for what America is, 'There definitely is a certain kind of stupidity that American culture has raised to a fine art. It's not an essence, but it is a phenomenon. Baudrillard again: leave irony to the Europeans; American art is best when it's like the desert or like crystal.' As for Kathy, riding free without a helmet on her motorbike, 'That's the decent side of the American nightmare,' that horror centre of what she calls the Aryan Nation, while affirming there are, fortunately, many different cultures. It's a complex picture she's part of, though needing the distance London gave her (a Bloomsbury crisis?). And of Australia? Well, at first: 'why Australia? I've never thought about Australia beyond having the usual friends who got drunk and ate

(143)

steak and eggs at five in the morning...(my first intro. to your countrymen)...'

Kathy visited Australia and you toured the bookshops together, spent three nights of which one was sexual discovery. Revelations, that's the compulsion. Kathy will say, a few days later in an email (was she drunk?—she is often drunk or wanting to eat breakfast: the time difference is the true essence of the temporal in this exchange...and then there's the long shadow of jetlag): 'I'm a total Romantic when let loose. And don't actually sleep around that much.' This is a Homeric catalogue of ships, tracking what might become of a relationship by noting what has come before and what will sail to Troy to seize (no rescue, I'm afraid) Helen back, to liberate the fetishised cunt (and still 'enjoy' the fetish), the working-through of what significant others have made of you, in you, of what you might be to each other. In it there are differing degrees of disclosure and intimacy, and always watch for that pirate's dagger in the back (antic-i-pation?).

In queering the turf, we look for liberation, for 'permanent liberation.' I was genuinely touched by your having to curl away, separate, to go to sleep, then in your sleep reaching across and making contact, and the bewilderment that it brings to Kathy. Those mixed signals. Those signals. Negotiations sleeping and awaking. Intimacy, and how much we can have of it and make of it, is at the core of this conversation, this exchange. The need for things to be outside conventions of gender and rage against PC formulations, to be the gays you both are and are not, but contest the bi as in-between. Mid 90s and I knew, as many others knew (growing to accommodate our desires and politics of un-hetero: our queering

(144)

into relationship), and so many of us wanted not to be anything but what we knew was the undoing of a dangerous 'man' politics.

But Kathy has the throbbing 'man motorbikes' between her legs, and transfers like that. She doesn't deny, just displaces, and you do in your way. The fist-fuck is not Pat Califia but Kathy Acker busting through the limits to the body's elasticity. You say Grace (your gender bête noire?) wouldn't stretch to it (though she dreams about it), but not for want of trying. Though there's a supreme affirmation of sex (Kathy: 'One can't argue solely from the rational, one has to account for experience, ESPECIALLY in the realm of the body. That's where sex so amazes me: what delights me is so often what I never suspected. And it may not again.'), surprisingly, so much of this isn't about sex per se, but just about love, and how friends who have just become friends position themselves for love. And sexuality here is a broad 'church' (playing with the sacred playing with itself), and the phallus is wondered-over, contested and as Ken (sorry, K, I am slipping into the infomercial mode: my epistle to you has become an analysis of 'you': Ken and Kathy) notes, 'I'm not often very dick-centred these days when I get horny.' There are many acts of curiosity, liberation and rejection in the affirming of a 'sexuality' and sexual practice.

But then you had a knowledge of Kathy long before, through her texts, and that's its own kind of intimacy. You already love or loathe or are indifferent to or curious about or maybe lust after the Acker of the page. In a vulnerable way, she'd expect it, surely. Your early letters have to work through this. Okay, you open a book of hers randomly and the opening is consolidated. I'll do the same:

(145)

> Finally, Pussycat and I were able to have sex.
>
> I talked to her for hours because I was shy. Then she put an arm around me, my back to her. We were sitting together on a crumbled wall by a duck pond. Dead ducks. I turned around and kissed her, I think because I have been waiting to for a long time and because I believed that I was supposed to and because I wanted her.

I find so much of this in your exchange. Supposed to and wanting to: negotiating the matrix of formative relationships. As you know, the book from which this is quoted was published in 1996. Its formulation is concurrent with you. With recording. With the Mekons. With San Francisco. With teaching and travelling and friendships coming in and out of focus.

And she read your *Virtual Geography* on the plane back, and dipped in here and there and in a slightly intimidated way, wondering whom she had slept with. She liked the risk, but felt the pain of uncertainty. A shift in the masochist need and 'repeller' (those strange attractors again). I love the stripping away, the gradual unmasking as you both work out how to go about it. Sometimes you're just blunt or matter-of-fact in the way you state things (yes, the medium, the medium: I love its prompts to terseness) and she takes it as rejection: she doesn't need all that information about previous 'rivals,' but she ultimately craves it because it's a spatial process as well as temporal. All that distance between you, then you'll be in San Francisco, but only long enough to get over jetlag because the tickets were booked before you met and she's onto the case, and you are too. I open my own signed copy semi-randomly. That's because I have three markers in there from the last time I was reading the book. I go for the second marker and open to page 194, and read the last paragraph which begins, 'This space of calculation is what Alain Lipietz, following Marx, calls the "enchanted world."' It is the world of 'prices proposed, profits anticipated and wages demanded.' This zeroes in (binary) on one of my joys in the exchange: the negotiations of space. Kathy says 'I don't fit in,' working through her space, but you both create a space in which a very different 'enchantment' works against and concurrently with the economic. You depart from Lipietz in your struggle with the cartoon nature of language's translation of the body into script. You make good, ironically, with your strange but almost 'classical' narratology in the exchange: the revelation of character, the right amount of background detail, the conflicts and possible resolutions, the edginess (what will alcohol bring out!). Okay, I am stretching it here and shifting fact to metaphor, but remember the Philip K. Dick story 'Human Is,' where the replaced husband is so much better than the original, and parasitic colonisation is chosen by the wife because she is treated better. I get that both of you are wanting to be treated 'better' in all of this. Not necessarily in friendships or relationships, but in the way you negotiate your own private spaces, especially vis-à-vis public manifestations. You both stick your necks out and the chopper always, *always* comes down. There are good side-effects, but you don't know how or even if you want to hold on to them.

So when real friendship takes hold it becomes 'chatting'? That's more than gossip, but a close relative. It's exchange without overt fear of consequences. One can slip up a little and it will be

(147)

absorbed. And this all in a few days, really. But time will tell. This short email of Kathy's (though she refers to them at 'letters' at one point, and at others that you have the San Franciscan tendency towards rapid and tireless emailing) captures this for me: 'This is almost like chatting. I certainly don't expect to hear from you re Matias; it's just my habit of saying where I am cause I tour so much if I don't do that I'm sort of nowhere. I'll have to introduce you to motorcycles…one of the last myths left. Actually I think they're coming back. Perhaps what you're referring to as the sacred. / Cool re your comfort with books. I have thousands.'

There's a poetics at work. A group poetics—you and Kathy and whatever else comes into orbit (for Kathy, American wrestling as performance art)—but also your unique poetics of private-public space. In writing her songs for the Mekons, Kathy reached into lyricism and wished for fiction (though she was the most poetic-lyrical weaver and assembler!). You, Ken, have always been a poet in the way Warhol was a poet: making the media lyrical out-side itself. Borg-like: of the collective, but also something new and deeply persuasive. Yet not violent and invasive like the Borg—though that buys into issues of the communal, communism (as imagined by *Star Trek* script writers). What would Kathy have known of that—she didn't watch much television and was still wrestling with the idea of *The Simpsons* which you were consuming as TV dinner. Your lyrical insights and interludes, existing as response and as utterances of separation (briefly? you're doing it your way) from the collective you're inside, analysing: 'So it's not that male bodies have to die, but to some extent male bodies are a good basis for the ritual sacrifice of Man. It's one of the things drag

(148)

sometimes aspires to. It's a refusal that draw attention to what it refuses.' And it's not just a matter of 'doing it,' but being it! Lyricism is a song's negotiation of space, the utterance looking for its co-ordinates, where it will and won't reach, those private spaces (from cunts, anuses, and eyes of penises to mouth and ears; in those spaces inside the building and those nooks and crannies without) it might settle. I say this in response to your declaration to Kathy: 'I'm not really equipped as a writer to do stupid. But I can do lyricism—the flattening out of the surface of the prose to a simple emotion. Hide all the rest in the architecture.'

How much of this is wrestling with addictions: addictions of communication, exchange, and touch? Kathy is a sleep junkie as you are a news and media junkie. I was a *junkie* junkie (that most masturbatory of repetitions). That's my personal needle in the haystack, a kind of sideline that compels a narcissistic reading. Kathy would never be that sort of junkie she says, though her close friend is (good reason not to be). Sex as addiction? I don't think so, not really here, strangely. At times it's forensic. Kathy and privilege, Ken and the great emptiness of the failed sacred that needs to be filled remorselessly to keep away the fear, the shadow of the failed and absent god, the simulacrum (to embrace it). There are some issues over 'identity.' The need to 'misbehave' and discuss such compulsions? Of status and icons, Kathy notes re the *New York Review of Books*, 'I rant against this and *The Nation* but I read them religiously. Perverse.'

In the end, mostly what I love about this exchange are the questioning and the non-understandings. Of all the ability you share to bridge divides, you still struggle with the 'boy'/'girl' binary,

(149)

no matter how much you queer the turf, or are queered, or stand outside the queer. You are yourselves struggling with embodiment, exhibition, closure, privacy, ambition, disillusionment, thirst for knowledge, thirstlessness, desire for obliteration and deeply-felt cautions (whether admitted or not or admitted while not). And how much more are we (we boys, girls, non-boys and non-girls and boy-girls and de-boys and de-girls and all others equally as well), how much more are we to get, to understand. Kathy here: 'This is precisely what Blanchot is arguing against—he's saying that immanence is as belief a ground for totalitarianism. Why the fuck do men want to be "the king who doesn't die" (the false sign that hides the reality of the king-murder, the basis of society, according to Bataille)? This is what I don't get?' We might go with Kathy's thinking into the (discrete and ironic?) contradictions regarding power and hierarchies in Foucault's 'Rule of immanence': 'One must not suppose that there exists a certain sphere of sexuality that would be the legitimate concern of a free and disinterested scientific inquiry were it not the object of mechanisms of prohibition brought to bear by the economic or ideological requirements of power' (p. 98; *The History of Sexuality, Vol 1*, Penguin, 2008).

This is called a 'correspondence,' and I have used the term exchange. But there is a Baudelairean correspondence at work in the sensual co-ordinates of what has now become (through publication) an active but ultimately curatorial space: an artwork, of sorts. But as we near the end of the interaction as captured in the participants' own words, we have a return to the unconfigured anomalies of the beginning: the brief physical interaction that stimulated the exchange. Kathy and Ken (that's *you*, Ken: or Ken as *he* was, you were, back *then*) talk on the phone and we're without access to the words (and do we, anyway, really have access to all their written words during the timeframe of this correspondence?). Ken says, 'It was strange talking to you on the phone cause we've never done it, but it was really good to hear your voice again.' Again. And there's the connection: the viscerality of words, of the voice, of bodies, of embodiment in different spaces. Ken ultimately wants 'a little more of that intimacy, and the *possibility* of sex.' That also describes the act of reading for me, in so many ways.

Best,

JK

ABOUT THE AUTHORS

Kathy Acker was a novelist, essayist and performance artist whose books include *Blood and Guts in High School*, *The Childlike Life of the Black Tarantula*, *Empire of the Senseless*, *In Memoriam to Identity*, *Don Quixote*, *My Mother: Demonology*, and her last novel, *Pussy King of the Pirates*. Born and raised on New York's Upper East Side, she died of breast cancer in Tijuana, Mexico, in 1997.

McKenzie Wark is an Australian-born writer whose books include *Virtual Geography*, *A Hacker Manifesto*, *Gamer Theory*, *The Beach Beneath the Street*, *Telesthesia*, *The Spectacle of Disintegration*, and *Molecular Red: Theory for the Anthropocene*. He teaches at The New School in New York City.